READER'S DIGEST

QUOTABLE QUOTES®

WIT AND WISDOM FOR ALL OCCASIONS
FROM AMERICA'S MOST POPULAR MAGAZINE

 Reader's Digest

The Reader's Digest Association, Inc.
Pleasantville, N.Y. /Montreal

PROJECT EDITOR
Deborah DeFord

PROJECT ART EDITOR
Judy Speicher

RESEARCH EDITOR
Mark LaFlaur

Library of Congress Cataloging in Publication Data
Reader's digest quotable quotes : wit and wisdom for all occasions
   from America's most popular magazine.
           p.   cm.
   Includes index.
   ISBN 0-89577-925-0
   1.Quotations, English. I. Reader's Digest Association.
   PN6083.R43   1997
   082--dc20   96-34560

Printed in the United States of America

Ideas are like rabbits. You get a couple and learn how to handle them, and pretty soon you have a dozen.

—JOHN STEINBECK

TABLE OF CONTENTS

A Note from the Editors

"The only thing sure about luck is that it will change."

That quote from Bret Harte is as appealing today as when it ran in the very first appearance of Quotable Quotes® — in the May 1933 issue of *Reader's Digest*. Since then, thousands of quotes have graced the feature, delighting and inspiring generations of readers.

In a publication that prides itself on the art of condensation, the quotations in this popular collection represent the finest tradition of brevity: they package profound ideas in just a few words. In compiling this column, we search out quotes that are serious and those that are amusing. We look for provocative comments, well expressed, on universal themes. Ideal candidates can be contemporary or classic, timeless or topical, whimsical or earnest.

We cull quotes from a wide variety of sources — books, newspapers, magazines, television, radio, movies, the Internet, anywhere we come across a likely thought pithily expressed. And these gems have a life span that endures long after and far beyond their appearance in The Digest. They can be found on refrigerator doors, sprinkled into commencement speeches, enlivening sales pitches, wherever someone thinks they can do the most good. Humorists and social commentators have thrived on them. And more than a few have wound their way into a poignant eulogy.

By their very nature, Quotable Quotes beg to be repeated, whether you share them during trying times or use them to drive home a point. What you derive from Quotable Quotes is of course personal, yet these brief words can also serve as a bridge to connect people or ideas.

In Quotable Quotes you'll find the wit and wisdom of men and women from all walks of life and from all ages — from Benjamin Franklin to Colin Powell, Abraham Lincoln to Mother Teresa of Calcutta, Margaret Mead to Garrison Keillor. Read what they have to say. And enjoy it!

WITHIN OURSELVES

It is only with the heart that one can see rightly; what is essential is invisible to the eye.

—Antoine de Saint-Exupery,
The Little Prince

THE ADVANTAGE OF SOLITUDE . . .

1 Be able to be alone. Lose not the advantage of solitude.

—Sir Thomas Browne

2 When we cannot bear to be alone, it means we do not properly value the only companion we will have from birth to death—ourselves.

—Eda LeShan
in *Newsday* (Long Island, New York)

3 We visit others as a matter of social obligation. How long has it been since we have visited with ourselves?

—Morris Adler

4 We cannot confront solitude without moral resources.

—Honoré de Balzac
Madame de la Chanterie

5 The result of joining two solitudes will always be a greater solitude.

—Pedro Luis
Flores de Otuno

6 Solitude is a good place to visit but a poor place to stay.

—Josh Billings

7 The same fence that shuts others out shuts you in.

—Bill Copeland

There's one thing worse than being alone: wishing you were. 8

—Bob Steele

Loneliness and the feeling of being uncared for and unwanted are the greatest poverty. 9

—Mother Teresa of Calcutta

Of all things that can happen to us, triumph is the most difficult to endure when we are alone. Deprived of witnesses, it shrinks at once. 10

—Gabrielle Roy
La Detresse et L'enchantement

Our language has wisely sensed the two sides of being alone. It has created the word "loneliness" to express the pain of being alone. And it has created the word "solitude" to express the glory of being alone. 11

—Paul Tillich
The Eternal Now

The man who goes alone can start today; but he who travels with another must wait until the other is ready. 12

—Henry David Thoreau

What a lovely surprise to finally discover how unlonely being alone can be. 13

—Ellen Burstyn

1 Man loves company—even if it is only that of a small burning candle.

—Georg Christoph Lichtenberg

THE RIGHT MEASURE OF HIMSELF . . .

2 Fortunate, indeed, is the man who takes exactly the right measure of himself and holds a just balance between what he can acquire and what he can use.

—Peter Latham

3 Integrity is not a conditional word. It doesn't blow in the wind or change with the weather. It is your inner image of yourself, and if you look in there and see a man who won't cheat, then you know he never will.

—John D. MacDonald
The Turquoise Lament

4 Integrity has no need of rules.

—Albert Camus

5 We get so much in the habit of wearing a disguise before others that we eventually appear disguised before ourselves.

—Jim Bishop

6 We don't know who we are until we see what we can do.

—Martha Grimes
Writer's Handbook

7 What we must decide is how we are valuable rather than how valuable we are.

—Edgar Z. Friedenberg

8 Our credulity is greatest concerning the things we know least about. And since we know least about ourselves, we are ready to believe all that is said about us. Hence the mysterious power of both flattery and calumny.

—Eric Hoffer
The Passionate State of Mind

9 No one beneath you can offend you. No one your equal would.

—Jan L. Wells

10 The superior man is distressed by the limitations of his ability; he is not distressed by the fact that men do not recognize the ability he has.

—Confucius

11 No man, for any considerable time, can wear one face to himself and another to the multitude without finally getting bewildered as to which may be the true.

—Nathaniel Hawthorne

12 Maybe taking ourselves for somebody else means that we cannot bear to see ourselves as we are.

—Albert Brie
Le Devoir

1 Until you make peace with who you are, you'll never be content with what you have.

—Doris Mortman
Circles

2 If we have our own "why" of life, we can bear almost any "how."

—Friedrich Nietzsche

3 Man shies away from nothing as from a rendezvous with himself— which makes the entertainment industry what it is.

—Fritz Muliar

4 To have doubted one's own first principles is the mark of a civilized man.

—Oliver Wendell Holmes Jr.

5 When one is out of touch with oneself, one cannot touch others.

—Anne Morrow Lindbergh
Gift From the Sea

6 Everything that irritates us about others can lead us to an understanding of ourselves.

—Carl G. Jung
Memories, Dreams, Reflections

7 Fair play is primarily not blaming others for anything that is wrong with us.

—Eric Hoffer
Working and Thinking on the Waterfront

8 Our opinion of people depends less upon what we see in them than upon what they make us see in ourselves.

—Sarah Grand

9 One can only face in others what one can face in oneself.

—James Baldwin

10 I have had more trouble with myself than with any other man I have ever met!

—Dwight L. Moody

11 Being yourself is not remaining what you were, or being satisfied with what you are. It is the point of departure.

—Sydney J. Harris

12 People often say that this or that person has not yet found himself. But the self is not something that one finds. It is something one creates.

—Thomas Szasz
The Second Sin

13 You have to start knowing yourself so well that you begin to know other people. A piece of us is in every person we can ever meet.

—John D. MacDonald
introduction to *Night Shift*
by Stephen King

1 The best vision is insight.

—MALCOLM S. FORBES
in *Forbes* magazine

2 Men go abroad to wonder at the heights of mountains, at the huge waves of the sea, at the long courses of the rivers, at the vast compass of the ocean, at the circular motions of the stars; and they pass by themselves without wondering.

—ST. AUGUSTINE

3 If a man happens to find himself, he has a mansion which he can inhabit with dignity all the days of his life.

—JAMES A. MICHENER

4 No sooner do we think we have assembled a comfortable life than we find a piece of ourselves that has no place to fit in.

—GAIL SHEEHY

5 Not until we are lost do we begin to understand ourselves.

—HENRY DAVID THOREAU

6 You may find the worst enemy or best friend in yourself.

—ENGLISH PROVERB

7 Know yourself. Don't accept your dog's admiration as conclusive evidence that you are wonderful.

—ANN LANDERS

Be yourself. No one can ever tell you you're doing it wrong. **8**

—JAMES LEO HERLIHY

Often we change jobs, friends and spouses instead of ourselves. **9**

—AKBARALI H. JETHA
Reflections

Everybody thinks of changing humanity and nobody thinks of changing himself. **10**

—LEO TOLSTOY

Everyone complains of his memory, and nobody complains of his judgment. **11**

—FRANÇOIS DE LA ROCHEFOUCAULD

SO SOOTHING TO OUR SELF-ESTEEM . . .

Nothing is so soothing to our self-esteem as to find our bad traits in our forebears. It seems to absolve us. **12**

—VAN WYCK BROOKS
From a Writer's Notebook

I don't want everyone to like me; I should think less of myself if some people did. **13**

—HENRY JAMES

When we are confident, all we need is a little support. **14**

—ANDRÉ LAURENDEAU
Une Vie D'Enfer

1 We may not return the affection of those who like us, but we always respect their good judgment.

—Libbie Fudim

2 A man can stand a lot as long as he can stand himself.

—Axel Munthe

3 Misfortunes one can endure—they come from outside; they are accidents. But to suffer for one's own faults—ah, there is the sting of life.

—Oscar Wilde

4 We are all worms, but I do believe I am a glowworm.

—Winston Churchill

5 The most difficult secret for a man to keep is the opinion he has of himself.

—Marcel Pagnol

6 Appearances give us more pleasure than reality, especially when they help to satisfy our egos.

—Émile Chevalier

7 The ingenuities we practice in order to appear admirable to ourselves would suffice to invent the telephone twice over on a rainy summer morning.

—Brendan Gill

8 We have to learn to be our own best friends because we fall too easily into the trap of being our worst enemies.

—Roderick Thorp
Rainbow Drive

9 A human being's first responsibility is to shake hands with himself.

—Henry Winkler

10 If you want your children to improve, let them overhear the nice things you say about them to others.

—Haim Ginott

11 We appreciate frankness from those who like us. Frankness from others is called insolence.

—André Maurois

12 We probably wouldn't worry about what people think of us if we could know how seldom they do.

—Olin Miller

13 We judge ourselves by what we feel capable of doing, while others judge us by what we have already done.

—Henry Wadsworth Longfellow

14 Argue for your limitations and, sure enough, they're yours.

—Richard Bach
Illusions

15 Morale is self-esteem in action.

—Avery Weisman, MD

1 Lack of something to feel important about is almost the greatest tragedy a man may have.

—ARTHUR E. MORGAN

2 Once in a century a man may be ruined or made insufferable by praise. But surely once in a minute something generous dies for want of it.

—JOHN MASEFIELD

3 In the depth of winter I finally learned that there was in me an invincible summer.

—ALBERT CAMUS
Lyrical and Critical Essays

4 Self-respect is the fruit of discipline; the sense of dignity grows with the ability to say no to oneself.

—ABRAHAM JOSHUA HESCHEL

5 The better we feel about ourselves, the fewer times we have to knock somebody else down to feel tall.

—ODETTA

6 A man can't ride your back unless it's bent.

—REV. MARTIN LUTHER KING JR.

7 Never feel self-pity, the most destructive emotion there is. How awful to be caught up in the terrible squirrel cage of self.

—MILLICENT FENWICK

8 Self-pity in its early stages is as snug as a feather mattress. Only when it hardens does it become uncomfortable.

—MAYA ANGELOU
Gather Together in My Name

9 Trust yourself. You know more than you think you do.

—BENJAMIN SPOCK, MD
Baby and Child Care

IMAGINATION IS A GOOD HORSE TO CARRY YOU . . .

10 Imagination is a good horse to carry you over the ground—not a flying carpet to set you free from probability.

—ROBERTSON DAVIES
The Manticore

11 Imagination is the true magic carpet.

—NORMAN VINCENT PEALE

12 The man who has no imagination has no wings.

—MUHAMMAD ALI

1 Imagination offers people consolation for what they cannot be, and humor for what they actually are.

—ALBERT CAMUS

2 There are lots of people who mistake their imagination for their memory.

—JOSH BILLINGS

3 You can't depend on your judgment when your imagination is out of focus.

—MARK TWAIN

4 He who has imagination without learning has wings but no feet.

—JOSEPH JOUBERT

5 Imagination will often carry us to worlds that never were. But without it, we go nowhere.

—CARL SAGAN
Cosmos

6 Imagination is the highest kite that one can fly.

—LAUREN BACALL
Lauren Bacall, By Myself

7 Imagination is as good as many voyages—and much cheaper.

—GEORGE WILLIAM CURTIS

8 I believe in the imagination. What I cannot see is infinitely more important than what I can see.

—DUANE MICHALS
Real Dreams

9 The opportunities of man are limited only by his imagination. But so few have imagination that there are ten thousand fiddlers to one composer.

—CHARLES F. KETTERING

10 Imagination is more important than knowledge.

—ALBERT EINSTEIN

11 He turns not back who is bound to a star.

—LEONARDO DA VINCI

12 Perhaps imagination is only intelligence having fun.

—GEORGE SCIALABBA
in *Harvard* magazine

13 I doubt that the imagination can be suppressed. If you truly eradicated it in a child, he would grow up to be an eggplant.

—URSULA K. LE GUIN
The Language of the Night

14 One of the virtues of being very young is that you don't let the facts get in the way of your imagination.

—SAM LEVENSON

15 If one is lucky, a solitary fantasy can totally transform one million realities.

—MAYA ANGELOU

THE BEST REASON FOR HAVING DREAMS . . .

1 The best reason for having dreams is that in dreams no reasons are necessary.

—ASHLEIGH BRILLIANT

2 There are no rules of architecture for a castle in the clouds.

—G. K. CHESTERTON

3 Hold fast to dreams/For if dreams die,
Life is a broken-winged bird/That cannot fly.

—LANGSTON HUGHES
The Dream Keeper and Other Poems

4 No bird soars too high if he soars with his own wings.

—WILLIAM BLAKE

5 The best way to make your dreams come true is to wake up.

—J. M. POWER

6 Nothing happens unless first a dream.

—CARL SANDBURG
Slabs of the Sunburnt West

7 A rock pile ceases to be a rock pile the moment a single man contemplates it, bearing within him the image of a cathedral.

—ANTOINE DE SAINT-EXUPÉRY
Flight to Arras

8 To fulfill a dream, to be allowed to sweat over lonely labor, to be given a chance to create, is the meat and potatoes of life. The money is the gravy.

—BETTE DAVIS
The Lonely Life

9 The years forever fashion new dreams when old ones go. God pity a one-dream man!

—ROBERT GODDARD

10 A man must have his dreams— memory dreams of the past and eager dreams of the future. I never want to stop reaching for new goals.

—MAURICE CHEVALIER

11 Dreams and dedication are a powerful combination.

—WILLIAM LONGGOOD
Voices from the Earth

12 I like the dreams of the future better than the history of the past.

—THOMAS JEFFERSON

13 We all live under the same sky, but we don't have the same horizon.

—KONRAD ADENAUER

1 The moment after Christmas every child thinks of his birthday.
—STEPHEN UYS

2 Everything starts as somebody's daydream.
—LARRY NIVEN
Niven's Laws

3 Rose-colored glasses are never made in bifocals. Nobody wants to read the small print in dreams.
—ANN LANDERS

4 How many of our daydreams would darken into nightmares, were there a danger of their coming true!
—LOGAN PEARSALL SMITH
Afterthoughts

5 Dreaming permits each and every one of us to be safely insane every night of the week.
—DR. CHARLES FISHER

ESTABLISHING GOALS IS ALL RIGHT . . .

6 Establishing goals is all right if you don't let them deprive you of interesting detours.
—DOUG LARSON

7 Discipline is remembering what you want.
—DAVID CAMPBELL

Goals are dreams with deadlines. 8
—DIANA SCHARF HUNT

The trouble with not having a 9 goal is that you can spend your life running up and down the field and never scoring.
—BILL COPELAND

In the long run men hit only what 10 they aim at.
—HENRY DAVID THOREAU

Don't bunt. Aim out of the ballpark. 11
—DAVID OGILVY

Aim at Heaven and you will get 12 Earth thrown in. Aim at Earth and you get neither.
—C. S. LEWIS

Keep high aspirations, moderate 13 expectations and small needs.
—H. STEIN

Goals determine what you're 14 going to be.
—JULIUS ERVING

The trouble with our age is that it 15 is all signposts and no destination.
—*The War Cry*

To live only for some future goal is 16 shallow. It's the sides of the mountain that sustain life, not the top.
—ROBERT M. PIRSIG
Zen and the Art of Motorcycle Maintenance

1 When you aim for perfection, you discover it's a moving target.
—GEORGE FISHER

2 Intelligence without ambition is a bird without wings.
—C. ARCHIE DANIELSON

3 Whoever wants to reach a distant goal must take many small steps.
—HELMUT SCHMIDT

4 I've always wanted to be somebody, but I see now I should have been more specific.
—LILY TOMLIN

5 There is nothing worse than being a doer with nothing to do.
—ELIZABETH LAYTON

THE MOST IMPORTANT THINGS IN LIFE . . .

6 The most important things in life aren't things.
—Quoted in bulletin of The First Christian Church of Fairfield, Illinois

7 Origins are of the greatest importance. We are almost reconciled to having a cold when we remember where we caught it.
—MARIE VON EBNER-ESCHENBACH

8 To see what is in front of one's nose requires a constant struggle.
—GEORGE ORWELL

9 If people concentrated on the really important things in life, there'd be a shortage of fishing poles.
—DOUG LARSON

10 If you can play golf and bridge as though they were games, you're just about as well adjusted as you are ever going to be.
—Manitoba Co-Operator

11 The only person you should ever compete with is yourself. You can't hope for a fairer match.
—TODD RUTHMAN

12 The great thing in this world is not so much where we stand as in what direction we are moving.
—OLIVER WENDELL HOLMES SR.

13 To have more, desire less.
—Table Talk

14 When we have provided against cold, hunger and thirst, all the rest is but vanity and excess.
—SENECA

15 A glimpse is not a vision. But to a man on a mountain road by night, a glimpse of the next three feet of road may matter more than a vision of the horizon.
—C. S. LEWIS

16 The last thing one knows is what to put first.
—BLAISE PASCAL

1 We need to learn to set our course by the stars, not by the lights of every passing ship.
—GEN. OMAR N. BRADLEY

2 What was most significant about the lunar voyage was not that men set foot on the moon but that they set eye on the earth.
—NORMAN COUSINS

3 The hardest thing to learn in life is which bridge to cross and which to burn.
—LAURENCE J. PETER

4 Take your work seriously but yourself lightly.
—C. W. METCALF

5 If you treat every situation as a life-and-death matter, you'll die a lot of times.
—DEAN SMITH

6 Do not take life too seriously. You will never get out of it alive.
—ELBERT HUBBARD

7 It's a funny thing about life; if you refuse to accept anything but the best, you very often get it.
—W. SOMERSET MAUGHAM

8 It is not the man who has too little who is poor, but the one who craves more.
—SENECA

Think big thoughts but relish small pleasures. 9
—H. JACKSON BROWN JR.
Life's Little Instruction Book

To be upset over what you don't have is to waste what you do have. 10
—KEN S. KEYES JR.
Handbook to Higher Consciousness

The pursuit of perfection often impedes improvement. 11
—GEORGE WILL
in Newsweek

One cannot collect all the beautiful shells on the beach. One can collect only a few, and they are more beautiful if they are few. 12
—ANNE MORROW LINDBERGH
Gift from the Sea

Look at everything as though you were seeing it either for the first or last time. Then your time on earth will be filled with glory. 13
—BETTY SMITH
A Tree Grows in Brooklyn

Climb up on some hill at sunrise. Everybody needs perspective once in a while, and you'll find it there. 14
—ROBB SAGENDORPH

The man who can't dance thinks the band is no good. 15
—POLISH PROVERB

1 Nothing is so good as it seems beforehand.

—GEORGE ELIOT
Silas Marner

2 In order to maintain a well-balanced perspective, the person who has a dog to worship him should also have a cat to ignore him.

—*Peterborough Examiner*

CONSCIENCE IS THAT STILL, SMALL VOICE . . .

3 Conscience is that still, small voice that is sometimes too loud for comfort.

—BERT MURRAY
in *The Wall Street Journal*

4 Conscience is a small inner voice that doesn't speak your language.

—*Merit Crossword Puzzles Plus*

5 The ultimate test of man's conscience may be his willingness to sacrifice something today for future generations whose words of thanks will not be heard.

—GAYLORD NELSON
in *The New York Times*

Conscience is God's presence in man. 6

—EMANUEL SWEDENBORG

Reason deceives us; conscience, never. 7

—JEAN JACQUES ROUSSEAU

Conscience is a mother-in-law whose visit never ends. 8

—H. L. MENCKEN

A conscience, like a buzzing bee, can make a fellow uneasy without ever stinging him. 9

—*American Farm & Home Almanac*

The one thing that doesn't abide by majority rule is a person's conscience. 10

—HARPER LEE
To Kill a Mockingbird

The truth of the matter is that you always know the right thing to do. The hard part is doing it. 11

—GEN. H. NORMAN SCHWARZKOPF

To know what is right and not to do it is the worst cowardice. 12

—CONFUCIUS

Self-discipline is when your conscience tells you to do something and you don't talk back. 13

—W. K. HOPE

1 In matters of conscience, the law of majority has no place.
—MOHANDAS K. GANDHI

2 People who wrestle with their consciences usually go for two falls out of three.
—Los Angeles Times Syndicate

3 There is no pillow so soft as a clear conscience.
—FRENCH PROVERB

4 A long habit of not thinking a thing wrong gives it a superficial appearance of being right.
—THOMAS PAINE

5 A lot of people mistake a short memory for a clear conscience.
—DOUG LARSON

6 Many people feel "guilty" about things they shouldn't feel guilty about, in order to shut out feelings of guilt about things they should feel guilty about.
—SYDNEY J. HARRIS

7 A good conscience is a continual Christmas.
—BENJAMIN FRANKLIN

8 A man cannot be comfortable without his own approval.
—MARK TWAIN

WISDOM IS THE REWARD . . .

Wisdom is the reward you get for a lifetime of listening when you'd have preferred to talk. 9
—DOUG LARSON

No man was ever wise by chance. 10
—SENECA

It requires wisdom to understand wisdom; the music is nothing if the audience is deaf. 11
—WALTER LIPPMANN
A Preface to Morals

What we do not understand we do not possess. 12
—JOHANN WOLFGANG VON GOETHE

One of the functions of intelligence is to take account of the dangers that come from trusting solely to the intelligence. 13
—LEWIS MUMFORD

What the heart knows today, the head will understand tomorrow. 14
—JAMES STEPHENS

Science at best is not wisdom; it is knowledge. Wisdom is knowledge tempered with judgment. 15
—LORD RITCHIE-CALDER

Never mistake knowledge for wisdom. One helps you make a living; the other helps you make a life. 16
—SANDRA CAREY

1 "Next time I will . . ." "From now on I will . . ." What makes me think I am wiser today than I will be tomorrow?

—HUGH PRATHER

2 There is a great difference between knowing a thing and understanding it.

—CHARLES KETTERING WITH T. A. BOYD
Prophet of Progress

3 The day the child realizes that all adults are imperfect he becomes an adolescent; the day he forgives them, he becomes an adult; the day he forgives himself he becomes wise.

—ALDEN NOWLAN
Between Tears and Laughter

4 Everyone is a damn fool for at least five minutes every day. Wisdom consists in not exceeding the limit.

—ELBERT HUBBARD

5 Wisdom too often never comes, and so one ought not to reject it merely because it comes late.

—FELIX FRANKFURTER

6 The wise person questions himself, the fool others.

—HENRI ARNOLD

7 The most manifest sign of wisdom is continued cheerfulness.

—MONTAIGNE

8 The art of living consists in knowing which impulses to obey and which must be made to obey.

—SYDNEY J. HARRIS

9 Wisdom consists of the anticipation of consequences.

—NORMAN COUSINS
in *Saturday Review*

10 Wisdom is the quality that keeps you from getting into situations where you need it.

—DOUG LARSON

11 It is only with the heart that one can see rightly; what is essential is invisible to the eye.

—ANTOINE DE SAINT-EXUPÉRY
The Little Prince

12 The more a man knows, the more he forgives.

—CATHERINE THE GREAT

13 Keep me away from the wisdom which does not cry, the philosophy which does not laugh and the greatness which does not bow before children.

—KAHLIL GIBRAN

14 The best-educated human being is the one who understands most about the life in which he is placed.

—HELEN KELLER

1 It is easier to be wise for others than for ourselves.

—ALEKSANDR I. SOLZHENITSYN
The First Circle

2 People far prefer happiness to wisdom, but that is like wanting to be immortal without getting older.

—SYDNEY J. HARRIS

3 Learning sleeps and snores in libraries, but wisdom is everywhere, wide awake, on tiptoe.

—JOSH BILLINGS

4 Nothing in life is to be feared. It is only to be understood.

—MARIE CURIE

5 Discretion is knowing how to hide that which we cannot remedy.

—SPANISH PROVERB

THE FIRST SIGN OF MATURITY . . .

6 The first sign of maturity is the discovery that the volume knob also turns to the left.

—"SMILE" ZINGERS
in Chicago *Tribune*

7 Life begins as a quest of the child for the man and ends as a journey by the man to rediscover the child.

—LAURENS VAN DER POST
The Lost World of the Kalahari

8 A child becomes an adult when he realizes he has a right not only to be right but also to be wrong.

—THOMAS SZASZ
The Second Sin

9 Maturity is the ability to do a job whether or not you are supervised, to carry money without spending it and to bear an injustice without wanting to get even.

—ANN LANDERS

10 You are not mature until you expect the unexpected.

—Chicago *Tribune*

11 The young man knows the rules, but the old man knows the exceptions.

—OLIVER WENDELL HOLMES SR.

12 You're never too old to grow up.

—SHIRLEY CONRAN
Savages

13 You grow up the day you have your first real laugh—at yourself.

—ETHEL BARRYMORE

14 Age is a high price to pay for maturity.

—TOM STOPPARD

15 To exist is to change, to change is to mature, to mature is to go on creating oneself endlessly.

—HENRI BERGSON

1 Maturity begins when we're content to feel we're right about something without feeling the necessity to prove someone else wrong.

—SYDNEY J. HARRIS

2 Maturity is reached the day we don't need to be lied to about anything.

—FRANK YERBY

3 Maturity means reacquiring the seriousness one had as a child at play.

—FRIEDRICH NIETZSCHE

4 Youth is when you blame all your troubles on your parents; maturity is when you learn that everything is the fault of the younger generation.

—HAROLD COFFIN

AS WE GROW OLD . . .

5 As we grow old, the beauty steals inward.

—RALPH WALDO EMERSON

6 How old would you be if you didn't know how old you was?

—SATCHEL PAIGE

7 Whatever a man's age may be, he can reduce it several years by putting a bright-colored flower in his buttonhole.

—MARK TWAIN

8 When it comes to staying young, a mind-lift beats a face-lift any day.

—MARTY BUCELLA
in *Woman* magazine

9 It's easier to have the vigor of youth when you're old than the wisdom of age when you're young.

—RICHARD J. NEEDHAM
A Friend in Needham, or,
A Writer's Notebook

10 Adults are obsolete children.

—DR. SEUSS

11 We all wear masks, and the time comes when we cannot remove them without removing some of our own skin.

—ANDRÉ BERTHIAUME
Contretemps

12 After a certain number of years, our faces become our biographies.

—CYNTHIA OZICK
The Paris Review

13 The mask, given time, comes to be the face itself.

—MARGUERITE YOURCENAR
Memoirs of Hadrian

14 The secret of staying young is to live honestly, eat slowly and just not think about your age.

—LUCILLE BALL

1 If youth only knew; if age only could.

—HENRI ESTIENNE

2 When the problem is not so much resisting temptation as finding it, you may just be getting older.

—*Los Angeles Times*

3 The person who says youth is a state of mind invariably has more state of mind than youth.

—*American Farm and Home Almanac*

4 If you carry your childhood with you, you never become older.

—ABRAHAM SUTZKEVER

5 Most people say that as you get old, you have to give up things. I think you get old because you give up things.

—SEN. THEODORE FRANCIS GREEN

6 You don't stop laughing because you grow old; you grow old because you stop laughing.

—MICHAEL PRITCHARD

7 We are only young once. That is all society can stand.

—BOB BOWEN

8 I've always believed in the adage that the secret of eternal youth is arrested development.

—ALICE ROOSEVELT LONGWORTH

9 The joy that is felt at the sight of new-fallen snow is inversely proportional to the age of the beholder.

—PAUL SWEENEY

10 Age does not protect you from love. But love, to some extent, protects you from age.

—JEANNE MOREAU

11 Age appears best in four things: old wood to burn, old wine to drink, old friends to trust and old authors to read.

—FRANCIS BACON

12 Growing up is usually so painful that people make comedies out of it to soften the memory.

—JOHN GREENWALD

13 Old age lives minutes slowly, hours quickly; childhood chews hours and swallows minutes.

—MALCOLM DE CHAZAL

14 When I no longer thrill to the first snow of the season, I'll know I'm growing old.

—LADY BIRD JOHNSON

15 Just remember, when you're over the hill, you begin to pick up speed.

—CHARLES SCHULZ

1 People are living longer than ever before, a phenomenon undoubtedly made necessary by the 30-year mortgage.

—Doug Larson

2 There is always some specific moment when we become aware that our youth is gone; but, years after, we know it was much later.

—Mignon McLaughlin

3 It takes about ten years to get used to how old you are.

—Quoted by Raymond A. Michel
in *The Leaf*

4 Middle age is the time when a man is always thinking that in a week or two he will feel just as good as ever.

—Don Marquis

5 Middle age is the awkward period when Father Time starts catching up with Mother Nature.

—Harold Coffin

6 Middle age is when you begin to wonder who put the quicksand into the hourglass of time.

—*The Orben Comedy Letter*

7 Midlife crisis is that moment when you realize your children and your clothes are about the same age.

—Bill Tammeus
in Kansas City *Star*

8 Youth is when you're allowed to stay up late on New Year's Eve. Middle age is when you're forced to.

—Bill Vaughn

9 What most persons consider as virtue, after the age of 40 is simply a loss of energy.

—Voltaire

10 I don't know what the big deal is about old age. Old people who shine from inside look 10 to 20 years younger.

—Dolly Parton
in *Ladies' Home Journal*

11 I have no romantic feelings about age. Either you are interesting at any age or you are not. There is nothing particularly interesting about being old—or being young, for that matter.

—Katharine Hepburn

12 Old age is having too much room in the house and not enough in the medicine cabinet.

—Orben's Current Comedy

13 When grace is joined with wrinkles, it is adorable. There is an unspeakable dawn in happy old age.

—Victor Hugo

14 A young boy is a theory; an old man is a fact.

—Ed Howe

1 Never lose sight of the fact that old age needs so little but needs that little so much.
—MARGARET WILLOUR

2 The older I grow the more I distrust the familiar doctrine that age brings wisdom.
—H. L. MENCKEN
Prejudices

3 Wisdom doesn't necessarily come with age. Sometimes age just shows up all by itself.
—TOM WILSON

4 You can judge your age by the amount of pain you feel when you come in contact with a new idea.
—JOHN NUVEEN

5 Sometimes the child in one behaves a certain way and the rest of oneself follows behind, slowly shaking its head.
—JAMES E. SHAPIRO
Meditations From the Breakdown Lane

6 The best thing about being young is, if you had to do it all over again, you would still have time.
—SANDRA CLARKE

7 If life were just, we would be born old and achieve youth about the time we'd saved enough to enjoy it.
—JIM FIEBIG

8 Everybody has been young before, but not everybody has been old before.
—AFRICAN PROVERB

9 You will stay young as long as you learn, form new habits and don't mind being contradicted.
—MARIE VON EBNER-ESCHENBACH

10 You are young at any age if you are planning for tomorrow.
—*The Sword of the Lord*

11 A grownup is a child with layers on.
—WOODY HARRELSON

12 When people tell you how young you look, they are also telling you how old you are.
—CARY GRANT

13 To age with dignity and with courage cuts close to what it is to be a man.
—ROGER KAHN

14 I speak truth, not so much as I would, but as much as I dare; and I dare a little the more, as I grow older.
—MONTAIGNE

15 The older you get, the more important it is not to act your age.
—ASHLEIGH BRILLIANT

1 The trick is growing up without growing old.

—CASEY STENGEL

2 Growing older is not upsetting; being perceived as old is.

—KENNY ROGERS

3 The trouble with class reunions is that old flames have become even older.

—DOUG LARSON

4 A person is always startled when he hears himself seriously called an old man for the first time.

—OLIVER WENDELL HOLMES SR.

5 After thirty, a body has a mind of its own.

—BETTE MIDLER

6 We grow neither better nor worse as we grow old, but more like ourselves.

—MAY LAMBERTON BECKER

7 The best thing about growing older is that it takes such a long time.

—WALTERS KEMP

8 One advantage in growing older is that you can stand for more and fall for less.

—MONTA CRANE

9 The best birthdays of all are those that haven't arrived yet.

—ROBERT ORBEN

10 The older I grow, the more I listen to people who don't talk much.

—GERMAIN G. GLIDDEN

11 We've put more effort into helping folks reach old age than into helping them enjoy it.

—FRANK A. CLARK

MEMORY IS THE DIARY . . .

12 Memory is the diary we all carry about with us.

—OSCAR WILDE

13 Count reminiscences like money.

—CARL SANDBURG

14 It's surprising how much of memory is built around things unnoticed at the time.

—BARBARA KINGSOLVER
Animal Dreams

15 We do not remember days; we remember moments.

—CESARE PAVESE
The Burning Brand

16 The moment may be temporary, but the memory is forever.

—BUD MEYER

1 Don't brood on what's past, but never forget it either.

—Thomas H. Raddall

2 Recall it as often as you wish, a happy memory never wears out.

—Libbie Fudim

3 Each of us is the accumulation of our memories.

—Alan Loy McGinnis
The Romance Factor

4 One form of loneliness is to have a memory and no one to share it with.

—Phyllis Rose
in *Hers: Through Women's Eyes*

5 Memories are the key not to the past, but to the future.

—Corrie ten Boom with
John and Elizabeth Sherrill
The Hiding Place

6 May you look back on the past with as much pleasure as you look forward to the future.

—Quoted by Paul Dickson in *Toasts*

7 Keep some souvenirs of your past, or how will you ever prove it wasn't all a dream?

—Ashleigh Brilliant

8 To live without a memory is to live alone.

—Gilles Marcotte

9 There is no fence or hedge round time that has gone. You can go back and have what you like if you remember it well enough.

—Richard Llewellyn
How Green Was My Valley

10 Everybody needs his memories. They keep the wolf of insignificance from the door.

—Saul Bellow

11 Each day of our lives we make deposits in the memory banks of our children.

—Charles R. Swindoll
The Strong Family

12 You never know when you're making a memory.

—Rickie Lee Jones
"Young Blood"

13 Our memories are card indexes— consulted, and then put back in disorder, by authorities whom we do not control.

—Cyril Connolly

14 What is memory? Not a storehouse, not a trunk in the attic, but an instrument that constantly refines the past into a narrative, accessible and acceptable to oneself.

—Stanley Kauffmann
The New Republic

1 Memory is a child walking along a seashore. You never can tell what small pebble it will pick up and store away among its treasured things.

—PIERCE HARRIS
Atlanta Journal

2 I'm always fascinated by the way memory diffuses fact.

—DIANE SAWYER
in *TV Guide*

3 When I was younger, I could remember anything, whether it had happened or not.

—MARK TWAIN

4 You can close your eyes to reality but not to memories.

—STANISLAW J. LEC
Unkempt Thoughts

5 There are times when forgetting can be just as important as remembering—and even more difficult.

—HARRY AND JOAN MIER
Happiness Begins Before Breakfast

6 Remembering is a dream that comes in waves.

—HELGA SANDBUR
". . . Where Love Begins"

7 Memory is a complicated thing, a relative to truth, but not its twin.

—BARBARA KINGSOLVER
Animal Dreams

8 Recollection is the only paradise from which we cannot be turned out.

—JEAN PAUL RICHTER

9 The true tomb of the dead is the heart of the living.

—JEAN COCTEAU

10 There is something terrible yet soothing about returning to a place where you once lived. You are one of your own memories.

—MARY MORRIS
Crossroads

11 Some folks never exaggerate— they just remember big.

—AUDREY SNEAD

12 The older a man gets, the farther he had to walk to school as a boy.

—*Commercial Appeal*
(Danville, Virginia)

13 God gave us our memories so that we might have roses in December.

—JAMES M. BARRIE

14 No memory is ever alone; it's at the end of a trail of memories, a dozen trails that each have their own associations.

—LOUIS L'AMOUR
Ride the River

IF YOU'RE YEARNING FOR THE GOOD OLD DAYS . . .

1 If you're yearning for the good old days, just turn off the air conditioning.

> —GRIFF NIBLACK
> in Indianapolis *News*

2 We have all got our "good old days" tucked away inside our hearts, and we return to them in dreams like cats to favorite armchairs.

> —BRIAN CARTER
> *Where The Dream Begins*

3 Things ain't what they used to be and probably never was.

> —WILL ROGERS

4 Nostalgia is a file that removes the rough edges from the good old days.

> —DOUG LARSON

5 In the old days, when things got rough, what you did was without.

> —BILL COPELAND

6 Nostalgia is like a grammar lesson: you find the present tense and the past perfect.

> —*The United Church Observer*

7 The essence of nostalgia is an awareness that what has been will never be again.

> —MILTON S. EISENHOWER
> *The Wine Is Bitter*

8 There has never been an age that did not applaud the past and lament the present.

> —LILLIAN EICHLER WATSON
> *Light from Many Lamps*

9 Nothing seems to go as far as it did. Even nostalgia doesn't reach back as far as it used to.

> —*Changing Times*

10 You can clutch the past so tightly to your chest that it leaves your arms too full to embrace the present.

> —JAN GLIDEWELL
> in St. Petersburg *Times*

11 A trip to nostalgia now and then is good for the spirit, as long as you don't set up housekeeping.

> —DAN BARTOLOVIC
> KPUG-KNWR, Bellingham, Wasington.

12 The past should be a springboard, not a hammock.

> —IVERN BALL

13 The older you get, the greater you were.

> —LEE GROSSCUP

PEOPLE TOGETHER

" It's the things in common that make relationships enjoyable, but it's the little differences that make them interesting.

—TODD RUTHMAN

"

HOME IS A PLACE . . .

1 Home is a place you grow up wanting to leave, and grow old wanting to get back to.
—JOHN ED PEARCE
in Louisville *Courier-Journal Magazine*

2 The fireside is the tulip bed of a winter day.
—PERSIAN PROVERB

3 The home is not the one tame place in the world of adventure. It is the one wild place in the world of rules and set tasks.
—G. K. CHESTERTON

4 One of the oldest human needs is having someone to wonder where you are when you don't come home at night.
—MARGARET MEAD

5 The strength of a nation derives from the integrity of the home.
—CONFUCIUS

6 Where we love is home—home that our feet may leave, but not our hearts.
—OLIVER WENDELL HOLMES SR.

7 Where is home? Home is where the heart can laugh without shyness. Home is where the heart's tears can dry at their own pace.
—VERNON G. BAKER
in *Courant* (Hartford, Connecticut)

8 My home is here. I feel just as at home overseas, but I think my roots are here and my language is here and my rage is here and my hope is here. You know where your home is because you've been there long enough. You know all the peculiarities of the people around you, because you are one of them. And naturally, memories are the most important. Your home is where your favorite memories are.
—PIETER-DIRK UYS

9 A child on a farm sees a plane fly overhead and dreams of a faraway place. A traveler on the plane sees the farmhouse . . . and dreams of home.
—CARL BURNS
The Drug Shop

10 When you finally go back to your old hometown, you find it wasn't the old home you missed but your childhood.
—SAM EWING
in *National Enquirer*

11 The reality of any place is what its people remember of it.
—CHARLES KURALT
North Carolina Is My Home

12 A small town is a place where there is little to see or do, but what you hear makes up for it.
—IVERN BALL

1 A small town is a place where everyone knows whose check is good and whose husband is not.
—SID ASCHER

2 A place is yours when you know where all the roads go.
—Quoted by STEPHEN KING in *Down East*

3 There's nothing people like better than being asked an easy question. For some reason, we're flattered when a stranger asks us where Maple Street is in our hometown and we can tell him.
—ANDREW A. ROONEY
And More by Andy Rooney

4 A man travels the world over in search of what he needs and returns home to find it.
—GEORGE MOORE

5 Visitors should behave in such a way that the host and hostess feel at home.
—J. S. FARYNSKI

A TRUE FRIEND . . .

6 A true friend is one who overlooks your failures and tolerates your successes.
—DOUG LARSON

7 One does not make friends. One recognizes them.
—GARTH HENRICHS

8 In prosperity, our friends know us; in adversity, we know our friends.
—JOHN CHURTON COLLINS

9 Strangers are friends that you have yet to meet.
—ROBERTA LIEBERMAN

10 Lots of people want to ride with you in the limo, but what you want is someone who will take the bus with you when the limo breaks down.
—OPRAH WINFREY

11 I value the friend who for me finds time on his calendar, but I cherish the friend who for me does not consult his calendar.
—ROBERT BRAULT

12 It may be true that a touch of indifference is the safest foundation on which to build a lasting and delicate friendship.
—W. ROBERTSON NICOLL
People and Books

13 Getting people to like you is only the other side of liking them.
—NORMAN VINCENT PEALE

14 It's the things in common that make relationships enjoyable, but it's the little differences that make them interesting.
—TODD RUTHMAN

1 The only way to have a friend is to be one.

—RALPH WALDO EMERSON

2 Be slow in choosing a friend, slower in changing.

—BENJAMIN FRANKLIN

3 Don't make friends who are comfortable to be with. Make friends who will force you to lever yourself up.

—THOMAS J. WATSON SR.

4 The bird a nest, the spider a web, man friendship.

—WILLIAM BLAKE

5 True friendship is a plant of slow growth.

—GEORGE WASHINGTON

6 It takes a long time to grow an old friend.

—JOHN LEONARD
in *Friends and Friends of Friends* by
Bernard Pierre Wolff

7 The most called-upon prerequisite of a friend is an accessible ear.

—MAYA ANGELOU
The Heart of a Woman

8 Men kick friendship around like a football, but it doesn't seem to crack. Women treat it like glass and it goes to pieces.

—ANNE MORROW LINDBERGH

9 Could we see when and where we are to meet again, we would be more tender when we bid our friends good by.

—MARIE LOUISE DE LA RAMÉE

10 Friends are relatives you make for yourself.

—EUSTACHE DESCHAMPS

11 The golden rule of friendship is to listen to others as you would have them listen to you.

—DAVID AUGSBURGER

12 You can make more friends in a month by being interested in them than in ten years by trying to get them interested in you.

—CHARLES L. ALLEN
Roads to Radiant Living

13 We need old friends to help us grow old and new friends to help us stay young.

—LETTY COTTIN POGREBIN
Among Friends

14 If you want an accounting of your worth, count your friends.

—MERRY BROWNE
in *National Enquirer*

15 My friends are my estate. Forgive me then the avarice to hoard them!

—EMILY DICKINSON

1 Friendship is a single soul dwelling in two bodies.

—ARISTOTLE

2 In my friend, I find a second self.

—ISABEL NORTON

3 No man is the whole of himself; his friends are the rest of him.

—HARRY EMERSON FOSDICK

4 Friendships multiply joys and divide griefs.

—H. G. BOHN

5 A friend is someone you can do nothing with, and enjoy it.

—The Optimist Magazine

6 We cherish our friends not for their ability to amuse us, but for our ability to amuse them.

—EVELYN WAUGH

7 A loyal friend laughs at your jokes when they're not so good, and sympathizes with your problems when they're not so bad.

—ARNOLD H. GLASOW
in The Wall Street Journal

8 How rare and wonderful is that flash of a moment when we realize we have discovered a friend.

—WILLIAM ROTSLER

9 To a friend's house, the road is never long.

—ANONYMOUS

10 A friend hears the song in my heart and sings it to me when my memory fails.

—Pioneer Girls Leaders' Handbook

11 True friendship is like phosphorescence—it glows best when the world around you goes dark.

—DENISE MARTIN

12 The proper office of a friend is to side with you when you are in the wrong. Nearly anybody will side with you when you are right.

—MARK TWAIN

13 A true friend never gets in your way unless you happen to be going down.

—ARNOLD H. GLASOW

14 It is important for our friends to believe that we are unreservedly frank with them, and important to friendship that we are not.

—MIGNON MCLAUGHLIN
The Neurotic's Notebook

15 The surest way to lose a friend is to tell him something for his own good.

—SID ASCHER

16 If it's painful for you to criticize your friends, you're safe in doing it; if you take the slightest pleasure in it, that's the time to hold your tongue.

—ALICE DUER MILLER

1 Only your real friends will tell you when your face is dirty.

—SICILIAN PROVERB

2 A friend is a lot of things, but a critic he isn't.

—BERN WILLIAMS

3 A friend is someone who can see through you and still enjoys the show.

—*Farmers Almanac*

4 Friends are those rare people who ask how we are and then wait to hear the answer.

—ED CUNNINGHAM

5 The most beautiful discovery true friends make is that they can grow separately without growing apart.

—ELISABETH FOLEY

6 Some of the most rewarding and beautiful moments of a friendship happen in the unforeseen open spaces between planned activities. It is important that you allow these spaces to exist.

—CHRISTINE LEEFELDT AND ERNEST CALLENBACH
The Art of Friendship

7 We love those who know the worst of us and don't turn their faces away.

—WALKER PERCY
Love in the Ruins

8 No man can be called friendless when he has God and the companionship of good books.

—ELIZABETH BARRETT BROWNING

9 An enemy who tells the truth contributes infinitely more to our improvement than a friend who deludes us.

—LOUIS-N. FORTIN
Pensées, Proverbes, Maximes

10 It pays to know the enemy—not least because at some time you may have the opportunity to turn him into a friend.

—MARGARET THATCHER
Downing Street Years

11 Pay attention to your enemies, for they are the first to discover your mistakes.

—ANTISTHENES

12 A friend is someone who makes me feel totally acceptable.

—ENE RIISNA

13 The best mirror is a friend's eye.

—GAELIC PROVERB

THE BEST HELPING HAND . . .

14 Sometimes the best helping hand you can get is a good, firm push.

—JOANN THOMAS

1 What do we live for if it is not to make life less difficult for each other?

—George Eliot

2 Whoever is spared personal pain must feel himself called to help in diminishing the pain of others.

—Albert Schweitzer
Memoirs of Childhood and Youth

3 Be not forgetful to entertain strangers: for thereby some have entertained angels unawares.

—Hebrews 13:2

4 No one is useless in this world who lightens the burden of it for anyone else.

—Charles Dickens

5 Great opportunities to help others seldom come, but small ones surround us every day.

—Sally Koch
in *Wisconsin*

6 I have always held firmly to the thought that each one of us can do a little to bring some portion of misery to an end.

—Albert Schweitzer

7 We ourselves feel that what we are doing is just a drop in the ocean. But the ocean would be less because of that missing drop.

—Mother Teresa of Calcutta

8 It is well to give when asked, but it is better to give unasked, through understanding.

—Kahlil Gibran
The Prophet

9 He who helps early helps twice.

—Tadeusz Mazowiecki

10 Expect people to be better than they are; it helps them to become better. But don't be disappointed when they are not; it helps them to keep trying.

—Merry Browne
in *National Enquirer*

11 You may give gifts without caring—but you can't care without giving.

—Frank A. Clark

12 Never hesitate to hold out your hand; never hesitate to accept the outstretched hand of another.

—Pope John XXIII

13 It is one of the beautiful compensations of this life that no one can sincerely try to help another without helping himself.

—Charles Dudley Warner

14 We love those people who give with humility, or who accept with ease.

—Freya Stark
Perseus in the Wind

1 Basically, the only thing we need
is a hand that rests on our own,
that wishes it well, that sometimes
guides us.
—HECTOR BIANCIOTTI
Sans La Misericorde du Christ

2 Extending your hand is extending
yourself.
—ROD McKUEN
Book of Days

3 The miracle is this—the more we
share, the more we have.
—LEONARD NIMOY

4 To ease another's heartache is to
forget one's own.
—ABRAHAM LINCOLN

5 The more sympathy you give, the
less you need.
—MALCOLM S. FORBES
in *Forbes* magazine

6 He is not an honest man who has
burned his tongue and does not
tell the company that the soup is
hot.
—YUGOSLAV PROVERB

7 Honesty is stronger medicine than
sympathy, which may console but
often conceals.
—GRETEL EHRLICH

8 Correction does much, but
encouragement does more.
—JOHANN WOLFGANG VON GOETHE

9 Money-giving is a good criterion
of a person's mental health.
Generous people are rarely men-
tally ill people.
—DR. KARL MENNINGER

10 The impersonal hand of government can never replace the helping hand of a neighbor.
—HUBERT H. HUMPHREY

11 You can't get rid of poverty by
giving people money.
—P. J. O'ROURKE
A Parliament of Whores

12 We'd all like a reputation for generosity, and we'd all like to buy it
cheap.
—MIGNON McLAUGHLIN

13 The greatest pleasure I know is to
do a good action by stealth and
have it found out by accident.
—CHARLES LAMB

14 Real charity doesn't care if it's tax-
deductible or not.
—DAN BENNETT

15 Criticism, like rain, should be
gentle enough to nourish a man's
growth without destroying his roots.
—FRANK A. CLARK

16 Nobody wants constructive criticism. It's all we can do to put up
with constructive praise.
—MIGNON McLAUGHLIN

1 The greatest good you can do
for another is not just to share
your riches but to reveal to him
his own.

—BENJAMIN DISRAELI

2 The pleasure we derive from
doing favors is partly in the feeling it gives us that we are not
altogether worthless.

—ERIC HOFFER

3 Deceiving someone for his own
good is a responsibility that
should be shouldered only by
the gods.

—HENRY S. HASKINS

4 Life's unfairness is not irrevocable;
we can help balance the scales for
others, if not always for ourselves.

—HUBERT H. HUMPHREY

5 We ought to be careful not to do
for a fellow what we only intend-
ed to help him do.

—FRANK A. CLARK

6 The more help a person has in his
garden, the less it belongs to him.

—WILLIAM H. DAVIS

7 The difference between a helping
hand and an outstretched palm is
a twist of the wrist.

—LAURENCE LEAMER
King of the Night

Few things help an individual 8
more than to place responsibility
upon him and to let him know
that you trust him.

—BOOKER T. WASHINGTON

Do not free a camel of the burden 9
of his hump; you may be freeing
him from being a camel.

—G. K. CHESTERTON

No matter what accomplishments 10
you achieve, somebody helps you.

—ALTHEA GIBSON

Do not commit the error, common 11
among the young, of assuming
that if you cannot save the whole
of mankind you have failed.

—JAN DE HARTOG
The Lamb's War

If you can't feed a hundred 12
people, then feed just one.

—MOTHER TERESA OF CALCUTTA

From what we get, we can make 13
a living; what we give, however,
makes a life.

—ARTHUR ASHE
Days of Grace

No person was ever honored for 14
what he received. Honor has been
the reward for what he gave.

—CALVIN COOLIDGE

1 The dead take to the grave,
clutched in their hands, only what
they have given away.
—DeWitt Wallace

2 The only things we ever keep are
what we give away.
—Louis Ginsberg
The Everlasting Minute and Other Lyrics

3 The fragrance always stays in the
hand that gives the rose.
—Hada Bejar

LOVE DOESN'T JUST SIT THERE . . .

4 Love doesn't just sit there, like a
stone; it has to be made, like bread,
remade all the time, made new.
—Ursula K. LeGuin
The Lathe of Heaven

5 In our life there is a single color,
as on an artist's palette, which
provides the meaning of life and
art. It is the color of love.
—Marc Chagall
Chagall

6 True love begins when nothing is
looked for in return.
—Antoine de Saint-Exupéry
The Wisdom of the Sands

7 At the touch of love, everyone
becomes a poet.
—Plato

8 This is the true measure of love:
when we believe that we alone
can love, that no one could ever
have loved so before us, and that
no one will ever love in the same
way after us.
—Johann Wolfgang von Goethe

9 Love does not consist in gazing
at each other, but in looking
outward together in the same
direction.
—Antoine de Saint-Exupéry

10 In the coldest February, as in
every other month in every other
year, the best thing to hold on to
in this world is each other.
—Linda Ellerbee
Move On: Adventures in the Real World

11 Only discretion allows intimacy,
which depends on shared reticence, on what is not said—
unsolvable things that would leave
the other person ill at ease.
—Hector Bianciotti
Sans La Misericorde Du Christ

12 We don't believe in rheumatism
and true love until after the first
attack.
—Marie von Ebner-Eschenbach

13 As soon go kindle fire with snow,
as seek to quench the fire of love
with words.
—William Shakespeare

1 I kissed my first woman and smoked my first cigarette on the same day. I have never had time for tobacco since.

—ARTURO TOSCANINI

2 All our loves are first loves.

—SUSAN FROMBERG
Schaeffer, Mainland

3 Two things only a man cannot hide: that he is drunk and that he is in love.

—ANTIPHANES

4 Is it not strange that love, so fickle, is ranked above friendship, almost always so worthy?

—GABRIELLE ROY
La Detresse et L'enchantement

5 Love is a game that two can play and both win.

—EVA GABOR

6 The giving of love is an education in itself.

—ELEANOR ROOSEVELT

7 We English have sex on the brain, which is not the most satisfactory place for it.

—MALCOLM MUGGERIDGE
in The Observer (London)

8 So many catastrophes in love are only accidents of egotism.

—HECTOR BIANCIOTTI
Sans La Misericorde Du Christ

9 Sometimes I wonder if men and women really suit each other. Perhaps they should live next door and just visit now and then.

—KATHARINE HEPBURN

10 You can't put a price tag on love, but you can on all its accessories.

—MELANIE CLARK

11 It is possible that blondes also prefer gentlemen.

—MAMIE VAN DOREN

12 Love is like quicksilver in the hand. Leave the fingers open, and it stays. Clutch it, and it darts away.

—DOROTHY PARKER

13 In true love the smallest distance is too great, and the greatest distance can be bridged.

—HANS NOUWENS

14 Love letters are the campaign promises of the heart.

—ROBERT FRIEDMAN

15 Only love can be divided endlessly and still not diminish.

—ANNE MORROW LINDBERGH

16 Love and time—those are the only two things in all the world and all of life that cannot be bought, but only spent.

—GARY JENNINGS
Aztec

1 It's easy to halve the potato where there's love.

—IRISH PROVERB

2 So long as we love we serve; so long as we are loved by others, I would almost say that we are indispensable.

—ROBERT LOUIS STEVENSON

3 The best proof of love is trust.

—JOYCE BROTHERS

4 Love is proud of itself. It leaks out of us even with the tightest security.

—MERRIT MALLOY
*Things I Meant to Say to You
When We Were Old*

5 Let there be spaces in your togetherness / And let the winds of the heavens dance between you.

—KAHLIL GIBRAN

6 Familiarity, truly cultivated, can breed love.

—JOYCE BROTHERS

7 Love is what you've been through with somebody.

—Quoted by JAMES THURBER in *Life*

8 Love is a fruit in season at all times, and within the reach of every hand.

—MOTHER TERESA OF CALCUTTA

9 Love is an image of God, and not a lifeless image, but the living essence of the all divine nature which beams full of all goodness.

—MARTIN LUTHER

10 Where there is great love, there are always miracles.

—WILLA CATHER
Death Comes for the Archbishop

11 The Bible tells us to love our neighbors, and also to love our enemies; probably because they are generally the same people.

—G. K. CHESTERTON

12 No disguise can long conceal love where it is, nor feign it where it is not.

—FRANÇOIS DE LA ROCHEFOUCAULD

13 We are shaped and fashioned by what we love.

—JOHANN WOLFGANG VON GOETHE

14 Him that I love, I wish to be free—even from me.

—ANNE MORROW LINDBERGH

15 No one worth possessing can be quite possessed.

—SARA TEASDALE

16 The ultimate test of a relationship is to disagree but to hold hands.

—Quoted by ALEXANDRA PENNEY in *Self*

1 The love of our neighbor in all its fullness simply means being able to say to him: "What are you going through?"

—SIMONE WEIL
Waiting for God

2 The worst prison would be a closed heart.

—POPE JOHN PAUL II

3 I love you, not only for what you are, but for what I am when I am with you.

—ROY CROFT

4 Tell me whom you love, and I'll tell you who you are.

—CREOLE PROVERB

5 Love at first sight is easy to understand. It's when two people have been looking at each other for years that it becomes a miracle.

—SAM LEVENSON

6 Love is not measured by how many times you touch each other but by how many times you reach each other.

—CATHY MORANCY

7 Nobody has ever measured, even the poets, how much a heart can hold.

—ZELDA FITZGERALD

8 Love is a great beautifier.

—LOUISA MAY ALCOTT

9 The purest affection the heart can hold is the honest love of a nine-year-old.

—HOLMAN F. DAY
Up in Maine

10 If only one could tell true love from false love as one can tell mushrooms from toadstools.

—KATHERINE MANSFIELD

11 Four be the things I'd have been better without: love, curiosity, freckles and doubt.

—DOROTHY PARKER

12 It is often hard to bear the tears that we ourselves have caused.

—*The Maxims of* MARCEL PROUST

13 Never close your lips to those to whom you have opened your heart.

—CHARLES DICKENS

14 To love and be loved is to feel the sun from both sides.

—DAVID VISCOTT, MD
How to Live With Another Person

15 Seek not every quality in one individual.

—CONFUCIUS

16 Love doesn't make the world go round. Love is what makes the ride worthwhile.

—FRANKLIN P. JONES

1 When one loves somebody, everything is clear—where to go, what to do—it all takes care of itself and one doesn't have to ask anybody about anything.

—MAXIM GORKY
The Zykovs

2 Love is like a violin. The music may stop now and then, but the strings remain forever.

—JUNE MASTERS BACHER
Diary of a Loving Heart

3 Love is an act of faith, and whoever is of little faith is also of little love.

—ERICH FROMM

4 Love endures only when the lovers love many things together and not merely each other.

—WALTER LIPPMANN

5 When a woman says, "Ah, I could love you if . . ."—fear not, she already loves you.

—WALTER PULITZER

6 A woman can say more in a sigh than a man can say in a sermon.

—ARNOLD HAULTAIN
Colombo's Canadian Quotations

7 We love because it's the only true adventure.

—NIKKI GIOVANNI

Love can achieve unexpected majesty in the rocky soil of misfortune. 8

—TONY SNOW
in Detroit *News*

Love is the magician that pulls man out of his own hat. 9

—BEN HECHT

There is no surprise more magical than the surprise of being loved. It is God's finger on man's shoulder. 10

—CHARLES MORGAN
The Fountain

To love is to admire with the heart; to admire is to love with the mind. 11

—THÉOPHILE GAUTIER

What the world really needs is more love and less paper work. 12

—PEARL BAILEY

Never look for a worm in the apple of your eye. 13

—LANGSTON HUGHES

Anything will give up its secrets if you love it enough. 14

—GEORGE WASHINGTON Carver

Love talked about can be easily turned aside, but love demonstrated is irresistible. 15

—W. STANLEY MOONEYHAM
Come Walk the World

1 The whole worth of a kind deed
lies in the love that inspires it.
—THE TALMUD

2 A baby is born with a need to be
loved—and never outgrows it.
—FRANK A. CLARK

3 I have enjoyed the happiness of
the world; I have loved.
—SCHILLER

A MARRIED COUPLE . . .

4 A married couple that plays cards
together is just a fight that hasn't
started yet.
—GEORGE BURNS
Gracie: A Love Story

5 Marriage resembles a pair of
shears, so joined that they cannot
be separated; often moving in
opposite directions, yet always
punishing anyone who comes
between them.
—SYDNEY SMITH

6 It isn't tying himself to one
woman that a man dreads when
he thinks of marrying; it's separating himself from all the others.
—HELEN ROWLAND
Violets and Vinegar

7 Marriage should be a duet—when
one sings, the other claps.
—JOE MURRAY

The value of marriage is not that 8
adults produce children, but that
children produce adults.
—PETER DE VRIES
The Tunnel of Love

Whoever thinks marriage is a 9
50–50 proposition doesn't know
the half of it.
—FRANKLIN P. JONES
in *Quote Magazine*

A marriage without conflicts is 10
almost as inconceivable as a
nation without crises.
—ANDRÉ MAUROIS
The Art of Living

A happy home is one in which 11
each spouse grants the possibility
that the other may be right,
though neither believes it.
—DON FRASER

More marriages might survive if 12
the partners realized that sometimes the better comes after the
worse.
—DOUG LARSON

One advantage of marriage is that, 13
when you fall out of love with
him or he falls out of love with
you, it keeps you together until
you fall in again.
—JUDITH VIORST
in *Redbook*

1 Marriage is a covered dish.

—SWISS PROVERB

2 Love, honor and negotiate.

—ALAN LOY MCGINNIS
The Romance Factor

3 Almost no one is foolish enough to imagine that he automatically deserves great success in any field of activity; yet almost everyone believes that he automatically deserves success in marriage.

—SYDNEY J. HARRIS

4 Marriage has teeth, and him bite very hot.

—JAMAICAN PROVERB

5 Getting married is easy. Staying married is more difficult. Staying happily married for a lifetime should rank among the fine arts.

—ROBERTA FLACK

6 Marriage is like vitamins: we supplement each other's minimum daily requirements.

—KATHY MOHNKE

7 Never marry for money. Ye'll borrow it cheaper.

—SCOTTISH PROVERB

8 A wedding anniversary is the celebration of love, trust, partnership, tolerance and tenacity. The order varies for any given year.

—PAUL SWEENEY

9 A good marriage is like an incredible retirement fund. You put everything you have into it during your productive life, and over the years it turns from silver to gold to platinum.

—WILLARD SCOTT
The Joy of Living

10 In every marriage more than a week old, there are grounds for divorce. The trick is to find, and continue to find, grounds for marriage.

—ROBERT ANDERSON
Solitaire & Double Solitaire

11 If you made a list of reasons why any couple got married, and another list of the reasons for their divorce, you'd have a lot of overlapping.

—MIGNON MCLAUGHLIN

12 The concept of two people living together for 25 years without a serious dispute suggests a lack of spirit only to be admired in sheep.

—A. P. HERBERT

13 Story writers say that love is concerned only with young people, and the excitement and glamour of romance end at the altar. How blind they are. The best romance is inside marriage; the finest love stories come after the wedding, not before.

—IRVING STONE

1 It takes a loose rein to keep a marriage tight.

—JOHN STEVENSON

2 The great thing about marriage is that it enables one to be alone without feeling loneliness.

—GERALD BRENAN
Thoughts in a Dry Season

3 A happy marriage is the world's best bargain.

—O. A. BATTISTA

4 Marrying for love may be a bit risky, but it is so honest that God can't help but smile on it.

—JOSH BILLINGS

5 The particular charm of marriage is the duologue, the permanent conversation between two people who talk over everything and everyone.

—CYRIL CONNOLLY
The Unquiet Grave

6 In marriage, being the right person is as important as finding the right person.

—WILBERT DONALD GOUGH

7 In a successful marriage, there is no such thing as one's way. There is only the way of both, only the bumpy, dusty, difficult, but always mutual path.

—PHYLLIS MCGINLEY
The Province of the Heart

8 Chains do not hold a marriage together. It is threads, hundreds of tiny threads, which sew people together through the years.

—SIMONE SIGNORET

9 All that a husband or wife really wants is to be pitied a little, praised a little, appreciated a little.

—OLIVER GOLDSMITH

10 Marriage should, I think, always be a little hard and new and strange. It should be breaking your shell and going into another world, and a bigger one.

—ANNE MORROW LINDBERGH

11 A happy marriage is a long conversation that always seems too short.

—ANDRÉ MAUROIS
Memoires

12 The difference between courtship and marriage is the difference between the pictures in a seed catalogue and what comes up.

—JAMES WHARTON

13 The greatest of all arts is the art of living together.

—WILLIAM LYON PHELPS
Marriage

14 A sound marriage is not based on complete frankness; it is based on a sensible reticence.

—MORRIS L. ERNST

1 A successful marriage requires falling in love many times, always with the same person.

—MIGNON MCLAUGHLIN
in *The Atlantic*

2 You don't marry one person; you marry three: the person you think they are, the person they are, and the person they are going to become as the result of being married to you.

—RICHARD NEEDHAM
You and All the Rest

3 Marriage is like twirling a baton, turning handsprings or eating with chopsticks. It looks easy until you try it.

—HELEN ROWLAND

4 The goal in marriage is not to think alike, but to think together.

—ROBERT C. DODDS

5 Married life teaches one invaluable lesson: to think of things far enough ahead not to say them.

—JEFFERSON MACHAMER

6 The marriages we regard as the happiest are those in which each of the partners believes that he or she got the best of it.

—SYDNEY J. HARRIS

7 Matrimony is the only game of chance the clergy favor.

—EMILY FERGUSON MURPHY

8 Nobody will ever win the battle of the sexes. There's too much fraternizing with the enemy.

—HENRY KISSINGER

THE GREAT GIFT OF FAMILY LIFE . . .

9 The great gift of family life is to be intimately acquainted with people you might never even introduce yourself to, had life not done it for you.

—KENDALL HAILEY
The Day I Became an Autodidact

10 A family vacation is one where you arrive with five bags, four kids and seven I-thought-you-packed-its.

—IVERN BALL

11 Family faces are magic mirrors. Looking at people who belong to us, we see the past, present and future. We make discoveries about ourselves.

—GAIL LUMET BUCKLEY
The Hornes: An American Family

12 Parentage is a very important profession; but no test of fitness for it is ever imposed in the interest of the children.

—BERNARD SHAW
Everybody's Political What's What?

1 A happy family is but an earlier
heaven.
—JOHN BOWRING

2 Other things may change us, but
we start and end with family.
—ANTHONY BRANDT
in *Esquire*

3 No matter how many communes
anybody invents, the family
always creeps back.
—MARGARET MEAD

4 Heredity is what sets the parents
of a teenager wondering about
each other.
—LAURENCE J. PETER
Peter's Quotations

5 Heredity is a splendid phenomenon that relieves us of responsibility for our shortcomings.
—DOUG LARSON

6 Adolescence is perhaps nature's
way of preparing parents to welcome the empty nest.
—KAREN SAVAGE AND PATRICIA ADAMS
The Good Stepmother

7 Few things are more satisfying
than seeing your children have
teenagers of their own.
—DOUG LARSON

8 Even a family tree has to have
some sap.
—Los Angeles Times Syndicate

9 Oh, to be only half as wonderful
as my child thought I was when he
was small, and only half as stupid
as my teenager now thinks I am.
—REBECCA RICHARDS

10 We never know the love of the
parent until we become parents
ourselves.
—HENRY WARD BEECHER

11 He that has no fools, knaves nor
beggars in his family was begot
by a flash of lightning.
—THOMAS FULLER

12 If you don't believe in ghosts,
you've never been to a family
reunion.
—ASHLEIGH BRILLIANT

13 Before most people start boasting
about their family tree, they usually do a good pruning job.
—O. A. BATTISTA

14 There is no king who has not had
a slave among his ancestors, and
no slave who has not had a king
among his.
—HELEN KELLER

15 The family fireside is the best of
schools.
—ARNOLD H. GLASOW

1 Making the decision to have a child—it's momentous. It is to decide forever to have your heart go walking around outside your body.

—ELIZABETH STONE

2 When you are a mother, you are never really alone in your thoughts. A mother always has to think twice, once for herself and once for her child.

—SOPHIA LOREN
Women and Beauty

3 Mothers are the most instinctive philosophers.

—HARRIET BEECHER STOWE

4 Instant availability without continuous presence is probably the best role a mother can play.

—LOTTE BAILYN
The Woman in America

5 The three most beautiful sights: a potato garden in bloom, a ship in sail, a woman after the birth of her child.

—IRISH PROVERB

6 Every parent is at some time the father of the unreturned prodigal, with nothing to do but keep his house open to hope.

—JOHN CIARDI

7 You never get over being a child, long as you have a mother to go to.

—SARAH ORNE JEWETT

8 A good father is a little bit of a mother.

—LEE SALK

9 The most important thing a father can do for his children is to love their mother.

—THEODORE HESBURGH

10 One father is more than a hundred schoolmasters.

—GEORGE HERBERT

11 My father didn't tell me how to live; he lived, and let me watch him do it.

—CLARENCE BUDINGTON KELLAND

12 You don't raise heroes; you raise sons. And if you treat them like sons, they'll turn out to be heroes, even if it's just in your own eyes.

—WALTER SCHIRRA SR.

13 The beauty of "spacing" children many years apart lies in the fact that parents have time to learn the mistakes that were made with the older ones—which permits them to make exactly the opposite mistakes with the younger ones.

—SYDNEY J. HARRIS

1 The thorn from the bush one has planted, nourished and pruned, pricks most deeply and draws more blood.

—MAYA ANGELOU
All God's Children Need Traveling Shoes

2 It doesn't matter who my father was; it matters who I remember he was.

—ANNE SEXTON

3 Parenthood remains the greatest single preserve of the amateur.

—ALVIN TOFFLER
Future Shock

4 The word no carries a lot more meaning when spoken by a parent who also knows how to say yes.

—JOYCE MAYNARD
in *Parenting*

5 Lucky parents who have fine children usually have lucky children who have fine parents.

—JAMES A. BREWER

6 Grandchildren are God's way of compensating us for growing old.

—MARY H. WALDRIP

7 Few things are more delightful than grandchildren fighting over your lap.

—DOUG LARSON

8 A grandmother is a person with too much wisdom to let that stop her from making a fool of herself over her grandchildren.

—PHIL MOSS
in *National Enquirer*

9 I have often thought what a melancholy world this would be without children—and what an inhuman world, without the aged.

—SAMUEL TAYLOR COLERIDGE

10 There's nothing like having grandchildren to restore your faith in heredity.

—DOUG LARSON

11 The simplest toy, one which even the youngest child can operate, is called a grandparent.

—SAM LEVENSON
You Don't Have to Be in "Who's Who" to Know What's What

12 Nobody can do for little children what grandparents do. Grandparents sort of sprinkle stardust over the lives of little children.

—ALEX HALEY
in *The Maroon*

13 I don't know who my grandfather was. I am much more concerned to know what his grandson will be.

—ABRAHAM LINCOLN

CHILDREN ARE THE LIVING MESSAGES . . .

1 Children are the living messages we send to a time we will not see.
—JOHN W. WHITEHEAD
The Stealing of America

2 My best creation is my children.
—DIANE VON FURSTENBERG

3 Every child comes with the message that God is not yet discouraged of man.
—RABINDRANATH TAGORE

4 Children are the anchors that hold a mother to life.
—SOPHOCLES

5 It is not easy to be crafty and winsome at the same time, and few accomplish it after the age of six.
—JOHN W. GARDNER AND
FRANCESCA GARDNER REESE
in *Know or Listen to Those Who Know*

6 Perhaps parents would enjoy their children more if they stopped to realize that the film of childhood can never be run through for a second showing.
—EVELYN NOWN

7 Cherishing children is the mark of a civilized society.
—JOAN GANZ COONEY

8 Human beings are the only creatures on earth that allow their children to come back home.
—BILL COSBY
Fatherhood

9 Life affords no greater responsibility, no greater privilege, than the raising of the next generation.
—C. EVERETT KOOP, MD

10 Children have more need of models than of critics.
—CAROLYN COATS
Things Your Dad Always Told You But You Didn't Want to Hear

11 The greatest natural resource that any country can have is its children.
—DANNY KAYE

12 Although today there are many trial marriages, there is no such thing as a trial child.
—GARY WILLS

13 Never worry about the size of your Christmas tree. In the eyes of children, they are all 30 feet tall.
—LARRY WILDE
The Merry Book of Christmas

14 In the little world in which children have their existence, whosoever brings them up, there is nothing so finely perceived and so finely felt as injustice.
—CHARLES DICKENS

1 Children are innocent and love justice, while most adults are wicked and prefer mercy.
—G. K. CHESTERTON

2 Children's talent to endure stems from their ignorance of alternatives.
—MAYA ANGELOU

3 When I was a child, love to me was what the sea is to a fish: something you swim in while you are going about the important affairs of life.
—P. L. TRAVERS

4 I still live in and on the sunshine of my childhood.
—CHRISTIAN MORGENSTERN

5 There are no seven wonders of the world in the eyes of a child. There are seven million.
—WALT STREIGHTIFF

6 The penalty for censoring what your children may be taught is children who are brighter than you.
—FRANK A. CLARK

7 If there is anything we wish to change in the child, we should first examine it and see whether it is not something that could better be changed in ourselves.
—CARL G. JUNG
The Development of Personality

8 Any child can tell you that the sole purpose of a middle name is so he can tell when he's really in trouble.
—DENNIS FAKES
Points with Punch

9 When I approach a child, he inspires in me two sentiments: tenderness for what he is, and respect for what he may become.
—LOUIS PASTEUR

10 We worry about what a child will be tomorrow, yet we forget that he is someone today.
—STACIA TAUSCHER

11 If children grew up according to early indications, we should have nothing but geniuses.
—JOHANN WOLFGANG VON GOETHE

12 A child is the root of the heart.
—CAROLINA MARÍA DE JESÚS

13 There never was a child so lovely but his mother was glad to get him asleep.
—RALPH WALDO EMERSON

14 Ask your child what he wants for dinner only if he's buying.
—FRAN LEBOWITZ
Social Studies

15 Telling a teenager the facts of life is like giving a fish a bath.
—ARNOLD H. GLASOW

1 Children have never been good at listening to their elders, but they have never failed to imitate them.

—JAMES BALDWIN

2 Oh, what a tangled web do parents weave when they think that their children are naive.

—OGDEN NASH

3 Babies are always more trouble than you thought—and more wonderful.

—CHARLES OSGOOD
"CBS Morning News"

4 The one thing children wear out faster than shoes is parents.

—JOHN J. PLOMP

5 Children aren't happy with nothing to ignore,
And that's what parents were created for.

—OGDEN NASH

6 Parents are the bones on which children cut their teeth.

—PETER USTINOV
in National Enquirer

7 Play is often talked about as if it were a relief from serious learning. But for children play is serious learning. Play is really the work of childhood.

—FRED ROGERS

8 Having a young child explain something exciting he has seen is the finest example of communication you will ever hear or see.

—BOB TALBERT

9 There's nothing that can help you understand your beliefs more than trying to explain them to an inquisitive child.

—FRANK A. CLARK

10 The greatest aid to adult education is children.

—CHARLIE T. JONES AND BOB PHILLIPS
Wit & Wisdom

11 Children are like wet cement. Whatever falls on them makes an impression.

—HAIM GINOTT

12 Children are not things to be molded, but are people to be unfolded.

—JESS LAIR

13 When everything is astonishing, nothing is astonishing; this is how the world is to children.

—ANTOINE RIVAROLI

14 You don't really understand human nature unless you know why a child on a merry-go-round will wave at his parents every time around—and why his parents will always wave back.

—WILLIAM D. TAMMEUS

1 A child is not a vase to be filled,
but a fire to be lit.
—RABELAIS

2 Kids are always the only future
the human race has.
—WILLIAM SAROYAN

3 The most important thing that parents can teach their children is
how to get along without them.
—FRANK A. CLARK

4 We set standards for drugs,
because bad drugs cross state
lines. Well, badly educated children cross state lines, too.
—ADM. HYMAN G. RICKOVER

5 If you want your children to keep
their feet on the ground, put some
responsibility on their shoulders.
—ABIGAIL VAN BUREN

6 Loving a child doesn't mean giving in to all his whims; to love
him is to bring out the best in
him, to teach him to love what is
difficult.
—NADIA BOULANGER

7 The best things you can give children, next to good habits, are
good memories.
—SYDNEY J. HARRIS

8 A child, like your stomach, doesn't
need all you can afford to give it.
—FRANK A. CLARK

9 The best security blanket a child
can have is parents who respect
each other.
—JAN BLAUSTONE
The Joy of Parenthood

10 The best inheritance a parent can
give his children is a few minutes
of his time each day.
—O. A. BATTISTA

11 Any kid who has two parents who
are interested in him and has a
houseful of books isn't poor.
—SAM LEVENSON

12 Sometimes the poorest man
leaves his children the richest
inheritance.
—RUTH E. RENKEL
in *National Enquirer*

13 The greatest gifts you can give
your children are the roots of
responsibility and the wings of
independence.
—DENIS WAITLEY

14 A truly rich man is one whose
children run into his arms when
his hands are empty.
—*Spotlight* (Boise, Idaho)

15 I have found that the best way to
give advice to your children is to
find out what they want, and then
advise them to do it.
—HARRY S. TRUMAN

1 If a child lives with approval, he learns to like himself.

—Dorothy Law Nolte

2 Parents need to fill a child's bucket of self-esteem so high that the rest of the world can't poke enough holes in it to drain it dry.

—Alvin Price

3 Every adult needs a child to teach; it's the way adults learn.

—Frank A. Clark

4 Children are likely to live up to what you believe of them.

—Lady Bird Johnson

5 If you can't hold children in your arms, please hold them in your heart.

—Mother Clara Hale

6 You cannot train a horse with shouts and expect it to obey a whisper.

—Dagobert D. Runes
Letters to My Son

7 What's done to children, they will do to society.

—Dr. Karl Menninger

8 What a father says to his children is not heard by the world; but it will be heard by posterity.

—Jean Paul Richter

9 Never fear spoiling children by making them too happy. Happiness is the atmosphere in which all good affections grow.

—Thomas Bray

10 The only thing worth stealing is a kiss from a sleeping child.

—Joe Houldsworth

MANNERS ARE THE HAPPY WAY . . .

11 Manners are the happy way of doing things.

—Ralph Waldo Emerson

12 Manners are a sensitive awareness of the feelings of others. If you have that awareness, you have good manners, no matter what fork you use.

—Emily Post

13 Most arts require long study and application, but the most useful of all, that of pleasing, requires only the desire.

—Lord Chesterfield

14 Life is not so short but that there is always time for courtesy.

—Ralph Waldo Emerson

15 Politeness is the art of selecting among one's real thoughts.

—Madame de Staël

1 To have a respect for ourselves guides our morals; to have a deference for others governs our manners.

—LAURENCE STERNE

2 Manners are like the zero in arithmetic; they may not be much in themselves, but they are capable of adding a great deal to the value of everything else.

—FREYA STARK
The Journey's Echo

3 Etiquette is getting sleepy in company and not showing it.

—HYMAN MAXWELL BERSTON

4 You can get through life with bad manners, but it's easier with good manners.

—LILLIAN GISH

5 Diplomacy gets you out of what tact would have kept you out of.

—BRIAN BOWLING

6 The point of tact is not sharp.

—COLLEEN CARNEY

7 People with tact have less to retract.

—ARNOLD H. GLASOW

8 Tact consists in knowing how far we may go too far.

—JEAN COCTEAU
A Call to Order

9 Tact is the knack of making a point without making an enemy.

—HOWARD W. NEWTON

10 Tact is the art of making guests feel at home when that's really where you wish they were.

—GEORGE E. BERGMAN
in *Good Housekeeping*

11 Tact is rubbing out another's mistake instead of rubbing it in.

—*Farmers' Almanac*

12 Tact is the art of recognizing when to be big and when not to belittle.

—BILL COPELAND

13 Tact is the ability to stay in the middle without getting caught there.

—FRANKLIN P. JONES

14 Tact is the art of convincing people that they know more than you do.

—RAYMOND MORTIMER

15 Tact is the art of building a fire under people without making their blood boil.

—FRANKLIN P. JONES

16 Never insult an alligator until after you have crossed the river.

—CORDELL HULL

1 The truly free man is he who knows how to decline a dinner invitation without giving an excuse.

—JULES RENARD

2 Every generation is convinced there has been a deplorable breakdown of manners.

—BYRON DOBELL
in *American Heritage*

3 To be agreeable in society, you must consent to be taught many things which you already know.

—TALLEYRAND

4 It takes a lot of thought and effort and downright determination to be agreeable.

—RAY D. EVERSON

5 Praise is like champagne; it should be served while it is still bubbling.

—*Robins Reader*

6 Charm is the quality in others that makes us more satisfied with ourselves.

—HENRI FRÉDÉRIC AMIEL

7 A gentleman is a man who uses a butter knife when dining alone.

—W. F. DETTLE

8 Nothing prevents us from being natural so much as the desire to appear so.

—FRANÇOIS DE LA ROCHEFOUCAULD

9 It is a great mistake for men to give up paying compliments, for when they give up saying what is charming, they give up thinking what is charming.

—OSCAR WILDE

10 Politeness is to human nature what warmth is to wax.

—ARTHUR SCHOPENHAUER

11 He who says what he likes, hears what he does not like.

—LEONARD LOUIS LEVINSON

12 The manner in which it is given is worth more than the gift.

—PIERRE CORNEILLE

13 To receive a present handsomely and in a right spirit, even when you have none to give in return, is to give one in return.

—LEIGH HUNT
Essays by Leigh Hunt

14 It is much easier to be a hero than a gentleman.

—LUIGI PIRANDELLO

15 Never claim as a right what you can ask as a favor.

—JOHN CHURTON COLLINS

16 To err is human; to refrain from laughing, humane.

—LANE OLINGHOUSE

OUR
BETTER SIDE

*Some people strengthen the society just by
being the kind of people they are.*

—JOHN W. GARDNER

A CONTINENT OF UNDIS-COVERED CHARACTER . . .

1 Every one of us has in him a continent of undiscovered character. Blessed is he who acts the Columbus to his own soul.

—Quoted in *Words of Life*, edited by Charles L. Wallis

2 Character is a strange blending of flinty strength and pliable warmth.

—ROBERT SHAFFER

3 No man knows his true character until he has run out of gas, purchased something on the installment plan, and raised an adolescent.

—EDNA MCCANN
The Heritage Book 1985

4 Character may be manifested in the great moments, but it is made in the small ones.

—PHILLIPS BROOKS

5 Nearly all men can stand adversity, but if you want to test a man's character, give him power.

—ABRAHAM LINCOLN

6 Everyone journeys through character as well as through time. The person one becomes depends on the person one has been.

—DICK FRANCIS
A Jockey's Life: The Biography of Lester Piggott

7 Character consists of what you do on the third and fourth tries.

—JAMES MICHENER
Chesapeake

8 You can measure a man by the opposition it takes to discourage him.

—ROBERT C. SAVAGE
Life Lessons

9 We know what a person thinks not when he tells us what he thinks, but by his actions.

—ISAAC BASHEVIS SINGER
in *The New York Times Magazine*

10 Another flaw in the human character is that everybody wants to build and nobody wants to do maintenance.

—KURT VONNEGUT
Hocus Pocus

11 Men are men before they are lawyers, or physicians, or merchants, or manufacturers; and if you make them capable and sensible men, they will make themselves capable and sensible lawyers or physicians.

—JOHN STUART MILL

12 The severest test of character is not so much the ability to keep a secret as it is, when the secret is finally out, to refrain from disclosing that you knew it all along.

—SYDNEY J. HARRIS

1 Show me the man you honor, and I will know what kind of man you are.

—Thomas Carlyle

2 People need responsibility. They resist assuming it, but they cannot get along without it.

—John Steinbeck
in *Saturday Review*

3 If anyone thinks he has no responsibilities, it is because he has not sought them out.

—Mary Lyon

4 Duty is a very personal thing. It is what comes from knowing the need to take action and not just a need to urge others to do something.

—Mother Teresa of Calcutta

5 Our concern is not how to worship in the catacombs, but rather how to remain human in the skyscrapers.

—Rabbi Abraham Joshua Heschel
The Insecurity of Freedom

6 The treacherous, unexplored areas of the world are not in continents or the seas; they are in the minds and hearts of men.

—Allen E. Claxton

7 The truth about a man is, first of all, what it is that he keeps hidden.

—André Malraux

8 Men show their character in nothing more clearly than by what they think laughable.

—Johann Wolfgang von Goethe

9 You can discover more about a person in an hour of play than in a year of conversation.

—Plato

10 There are two insults no human being will endure: that he has no sense of humor, and that he has never known trouble.

—Sinclair Lewis

11 Sports do not build character. They reveal it.

—Heywood Hale Broun

12 How a man plays the game shows something of his character; how he loses shows all of it.

—*Tribune* (Camden County, Georgia)

13 In our play we reveal what kind of people we are.

—Ovid

14 You can tell more about a person by what he says about others than you can by what others say about him.

—Leo Aikman

15 Character is what you know you are, not what others think you are.

—Marva Collins and Civia Tamarkin
Marva Collins' Way

1 You can easily judge the character of a man by how he treats those who can do nothing for him.

—James D. Miles

2 Character is much easier kept than recovered.

—Thomas Paine

3 The way to gain a good reputation is to endeavor to be what you desire to appear.

—Socrates

4 A good reputation is better than fame.

—Louis Dudek
Epigrams

5 Reputation is character minus what you've been caught doing.

—Michael Iapoce
A Funny Thing Happened on the Way to the Boardroom

6 Life is for one generation; a good name is forever.

—Japanese proverb

7 To have lost your reputation is to be dead among the living.

—S. H. Simmons

8 Modesty is to merit what shade is to figures in a picture; it gives it strength and makes it stand out.

—Jean de la Bruyère

9 Modesty is the clothing of talent.

—Pierre Veron

10 He who is slowest in making a promise is most faithful in its performance.

—Jean Jacques Rousseau

11 The only way to make a man trustworthy is to trust him.

—Henry L. Stimson
in *Harper's Magazine*

12 Willpower is being able to eat just one salted peanut.

—Pat Elphinstone

13 The best discipline, maybe the only discipline that really works, is self-discipline.

—Walter Kiechel III
in *Fortune*

14 You can find on the outside only what you possess on the inside.

—Adolfo Montiel Ballesteros
La Honda y La Flor

15 In great matters men show themselves as they wish to be seen; in small matters, as they are.

—Gamaliel Bradford

16 What lies behind us and what lies before us are small matters compared to what lies within us.

—Ralph Waldo Emerson

1 I see God in every human being.
—MOTHER TERESA OF CALCUTTA

2 Men may be divided almost any way we please, but I have found the most useful distinction to be made between those who devote their lives to conjugating the verb "to be," and those who spend their lives conjugating the verb "to have."
—SYDNEY J. HARRIS

3 There is more simplicity in the man who eats caviar on impulse than in the man who eats Grape Nuts on principle.
—G. K. CHESTERTON

4 One of the best ways to measure people is to watch the way they behave when something free is offered.
—ANN LANDERS

5 Say not you know a man entirely till you have divided an inheritance with him.
—JOHANN KASPAR LAVATER

6 Not what I have but what I do is my kingdom.
—THOMAS CARLYLE

7 The reputation of a thousand years may be determined by the conduct of one hour.
—JAPANESE PROVERB

Fame is the perfume of heroic deeds. 8
—SOCRATES

Dollars have never been known to 9 produce character, and character will never be produced by money.
—W. K. KELLOGG
I'll Invest My Money in People

One isn't born one's self. One is 10 born with a mass of expectations, a mass of other people's ideas— and you have to work through it all.
—V. S. NAIPAUL

Don't laugh at a youth for his 11 affectations; he is only trying on one face after another to find a face of his own.
—LOGAN PEARSALL SMITH

It has amazed me that the most 12 incongruous traits should exist in the same person and, for all that, yield a plausible harmony.
—W. SOMERSET MAUGHAM

We spend our time searching for 13 security and hate it when we get it.
—JOHN STEINBECK
America and Americans

Without heroes, we are all plain 14 people and don't know how far we can go.
—BERNARD MALAMUD
The Natural

1 The great man is he who does not lose his child-heart.

—MENCIUS

2 No great scoundrel is ever uninteresting.

—MURRAY KEMPTON
in *Newsday* (Long Island, New York)

3 Characters live to be noticed. People with character notice how they live.

—NANCY MOSER

4 Man is harder than iron, stronger than stone and more fragile than a rose.

—TURKISH PROVERB

5 He is ill clothed that is bare of virtue.

—BENJAMIN FRANKLIN

6 All of us are experts at practicing virtue at a distance.

—THEODORE M. HESBURGH

7 To err is human; to blame it on the other guy is even more human.

—BOB GODDARD

8 Man is the only kind of varmint sets his own trap, baits it, then steps in it.

—JOHN STEINBECK
Sweet Thursday

9 There's man all over for you, blaming on his boots the faults of his feet.

—SAMUEL BECKETT
Waiting for Godot

AN OPTIMIST STAYS UP UNTIL MIDNIGHT . . .

10 An optimist stays up until midnight to see the new year in. A pessimist stays up to make sure the old year leaves.

—BILL VAUGHAN
in Kansas City *Star*

11 Perpetual optimism is a force multiplier.

—COLIN POWELL

12 I will say this about being an optimist—even when things don't turn out well, you are certain they will get better.

—FRANK HUGHES

13 An optimist thinks this is the best of all worlds. A pessimist fears the same may be true.

—DOUG LARSON

14 Things will probably come out all right, but sometimes it takes strong nerves just to watch.

—HEDLEY DONOVAN

1 The optimist already sees the scar over the wound; the pessimist still sees the wound underneath the scar.

—ERNST SCHRODER

2 The point of living, and of being an optimist, is to be foolish enough to believe the best is yet to come.

—PETER USTINOV

3 It doesn't hurt to be optimistic. You can always cry later.

—LUCIMAR SANTOS DE LIMA

4 Cheerfulness, like spring, opens all the blossoms of the inward man.

—JEAN PAUL RICHTER

5 An optimist is the human personi-fication of spring.

—SUSAN J. BISSONETTE

6 I always prefer to believe the best of everybody—it saves so much trouble.

—RUDYARD KIPLING

7 A positive attitude may not solve all your problems, but it will annoy enough people to make it worth the effort.

—HERM ALBRIGHT

8 Optimism is an intellectual choice.

—DIANA SCHNEIDER

9 Optimism is a cheerful frame of mind that enables a teakettle to sing though in hot water up to its nose.

—Quoted by HAROLD HELFER in
The Optimist

10 An optimist is a person who starts a new diet on Thanksgiving Day.

—IRV KUPCINET
in Kup's Column

11 The average pencil is seven inches long, with just a half-inch eraser—in case you thought optimism was dead.

—ROBERT BRAULT

12 Both optimists and pessimists contribute to our society. The optimist invents the airplane and the pessimist the parachute.

—GIL STERN

13 A pessimist? That's a person who has been intimately acquainted with an optimist.

—ELBERT HUBBARD

14 Pessimism never won any battle.
—DWIGHT D. EISENHOWER

15 The nice part about being a pes-simist is that you are constantly being either proven right or pleasantly surprised.

—GEORGE F. WILL
The Leveling Wind

1 I don't believe in pessimism. If something doesn't come up the way you want, forge ahead. If you think it's going to rain, it will.

—CLINT EASTWOOD

2 No one really knows enough to be a pessimist.

—NORMAN COUSINS

3 The optimist is the kind of person who believes a housefly is looking for a way out.

—GEORGE JEAN NATHAN

4 The pessimist complains about the wind; the optimist expects it to change; the realist adjusts the sails.

—WILLIAM ARTHUR WARD

5 A pessimist sees only the dark side of the clouds, and mopes; a philosopher sees both sides, and shrugs; an optimist doesn't see the clouds at all—he's walking on them.

—LEONARD LOUIS LEVINSON

6 An idealist believes the short run doesn't count. A cynic believes the long run doesn't matter. A realist believes that what is done or left undone in the short run determines the long run.

—SYDNEY J. HARRIS

MORALITY IS ITS OWN ADVOCATE . . .

Morality is its own advocate; it is 7 never necessary to apologize for it.

—EDITH L. HARRELL

The three hardest tasks in the 8 world are neither physical feats nor intellectual achievements, but moral acts: to return love for hate, to include the excluded, and to say, "I was wrong."

—SYDNEY J. HARRIS
Pieces of Eight

Moral excellence comes about as 9 a result of habit. We become just by doing just acts, temperate by doing temperate acts, brave by doing brave acts.

—ARISTOTLE

It is much easier to repent of sins 10 that we have committed than to repent of those we intend to commit.

—JOSH BILLINGS

The biggest threat to our well- 11 being is the absence of moral clarity and purpose.

—RICK SHUMAN
in *Time*

We laugh at honor and are shocked 12 to find traitors in our midst.

—C. S. LEWIS
The Abolition of Man

1 It's discouraging to think how many people are shocked by honesty and how few by deceit.
—NOËL COWARD
Blithe Spirit

2 A good example is like a bell that calls many to church.
—DANISH PROVERB

3 One man practicing sportsmanship is far better than 50 preaching it.
—KNUTE K. ROCKNE
Coaching

4 The time is always right to do what is right.
—REV. MARTIN LUTHER KING JR.

5 Count no day lost in which you waited your turn, took only your share and sought advantage over no one.
—ROBERT BRAULT

6 The glory of great men should always be measured by the means they have used to acquire it.
—FRANÇOIS DE LA ROCHEFOUCAULD

7 To have a right to do a thing is not at all the same as to be right in doing it.
—G. K. CHESTERTON

8 If you're going to do something tonight that you'll be sorry for tomorrow morning, sleep late.
—HENNY YOUNGMAN

9 Be on guard against excess. Zeal that is too ardent burns more than it reheats.
—ALEC PELLETIER
Le Festin des Morts

10 What is right is often forgotten by what is convenient.
—BODIE THOENE
Warsaw Requiem

11 The arm of the moral universe is long, but it bends toward justice.
—REV. MARTIN LUTHER KING JR.

12 If you don't want anyone to know, don't do it.
—CHINESE PROVERB

13 No virtue can be great if it is not constant.
—ALFONSO MILAGRO
Los Cinco Minutos de Dios

14 Live so that your friends can defend you but never have to.
—ARNOLD H. GLASOW
in *Forbes* magazine

15 Always put off until tomorrow what you shouldn't do at all.
—MORRIS MANDEL

16 You can't run a society or cope with its problems if people are not held accountable for what they do.
—JOHN LEO
in *U.S. News & World Report*

1 Stigmas are the corollaries of values. If work, independence, responsibility, respectability are valued, then their converse must be devalued, seen as disreputable.
—GERTRUDE HIMMELFARB
The De-moralization of Society

2 The essence of immorality is the tendency to make an exception of myself.
—JANE ADDAMS

3 He who does not prevent a crime when he can, encourages it.
—SENECA

4 A sense of shame is not a bad moral compass.
—GEN. COLIN POWELL
My American Journey

5 One of the misfortunes of our time is that in getting rid of false shame we have killed off so much real shame as well.
—LOUIS KRONENBERGER

6 If moral behavior were simply following rules, we could program a computer to be moral.
—SAMUEL P. GINDER
in *Washington Post*

7 It is unwise to do unto others as you would that they do unto you. Their tastes may not be the same.
—BERNARD SHAW

8 What you dislike for yourself do not like for me.
—SPANISH PROVERB

9 Boredom is a vital problem for the moralist, since at least half the sins of mankind are caused by the fear of it.
—BERTRAND RUSSELL

THE PRINCIPAL MARK OF GENIUS . . .

10 The principal mark of genius is not perfection but originality, the opening of new frontiers.
—ARTHUR KOESTLER
The Act of Creation

11 Originality is unexplored territory. You get there by carrying a canoe—you can't take a taxi.
—ALAN ALDA

12 The only real voyage of discovery consists not in seeking new landscapes but in having new eyes.
—MARCEL PROUST

13 You don't get harmony when everybody sings the same note.
—DOUG FLOYD
in *Spokesman Review*
(Spokane, Washington)

14 Since God made us to be originals, why stoop to be a copy?
—REV. BILLY GRAHAM

1 While an original is always hard to find, he is easy to recognize.
—JOHN L. MASON
An Enemy Called Average

2 The courage to imagine the otherwise is our greatest resource, adding color and suspense to all our life.
—DANIEL J. BOORSTIN

3 Discoveries are often made by not following instructions, by going off the main road, by trying the untried.
—FRANK TYGER
in *Forbes* magazine

4 It is by logic that we prove, but by intuition that we discover.
—HENRI POINCARÉ

5 Don't expect anything original from an echo.
—Quoted in "The 365 Great Quotes-a-Year Calendar"

6 Truth always originates in a minority of one, and every custom begins as a broken precedent.
—WILL DURANT

7 Eventually it comes to you: the thing that makes you exceptional, if you are at all, is inevitably that which must also make you lonely.
—LORRAINE HANSBERRY

8 If you're strong enough, there are no precedents.
—F. SCOTT FITZGERALD
The Crack-Up, edited by Edmund Wilson

9 The more original a discovery, the more obvious it seems afterward.
—ARTHUR KOESTLER
The Act of Creation

10 To go against the dominant thinking of your friends, of most of the people you see every day, is perhaps the most difficult act of heroism you can perform.
—THEODORE H. WHITE

11 Every society honors its live conformists and its dead troublemakers.
—MIGNON McLAUGHLIN

12 Everyone has talent; what is rare is the courage to follow the talent to the dark place where it leads.
—ERICA JONG

13 To do what others cannot do is talent. To do what talent cannot do is genius.
—WILL HENRY

14 When there is an original sound in the world, it wakens a hundred echoes.
—JOHN A. SHEDD
Salt from My Attic

1 The cynic says, "One man can't do anything." I say, "Only one man can do anything." One man interacting creatively with others can move the world.

—JOHN W. GARDNER

2 Everything has been thought of before, but the difficulty is to think of it again.

—JOHANN WOLFGANG VON GOETHE

3 Inspiration is never genuine if it is known as inspiration at the time. True inspiration always steals on a person, its importance not being fully recognized for some time.

—SAMUEL BUTLER

4 The work of the individual still remains the spark that moves mankind forward.

—IGOR SIKORSKY

5 The most powerful weapon on earth is the human soul on fire.

—FERDINAND FOCH

6 Whatever comes from the heart carries the heat and color of its birthplace.

—OLIVER WENDELL HOLMES SR.

7 We might define an eccentric as a man who is a law unto himself, and a crank as one who, having determined what the law is, insists on laying it down to others.

—LOUIS KRONENBERGER

8 No two men are alike, and both of them are happy for it.

—MORRIS MANDEL
in *The Jewish Press*

9 Some people march to a different drummer—and some people polka.

—Los Angeles Times Syndicate

THE REAL SECRET OF PATIENCE . . .

10 The real secret of patience is to find something else to do in the meantime.

—*Dell Pencil Puzzles and Word Games*

11 I endeavor to be wise when I cannot be merry, easy when I cannot be glad, content with what cannot be mended and patient when there be no redress.

—ELIZABETH MONTAGU

12 If you are patient in one moment of anger, you will escape a hundred days of sorrow.

—CHINESE EPIGRAM

13 He that can have patience can have what he will.

—BENJAMIN FRANKLIN

14 The key to everything is patience. You get the chicken by hatching the egg, not by smashing it.

—ARNOLD H. GLASOW

1 Patience! The windmill never strays in search of the wind.

—ANDY J. SKLIVIS

2 Nothing valuable can be lost by taking time.

—ABRAHAM LINCOLN

3 In any contest between power and patience, bet on patience.

—W. B. PRESCOTT

4 Beware the fury of a patient man.

—JOHN DRYDEN

5 Patience is bitter, but its fruit is sweet.

—JEAN JACQUES ROUSSEAU

6 Patience is the art of hoping.

—VAUVENARGUES

7 Be patient with everyone, but above all with yourself.

—ST. FRANCIS DE SALES

8 Patience is the ability to put up with people you'd like to put down.

—ULRIKE RUFFERT

9 There is a limit at which forbearance ceases to be a virtue.

—EDMUND BURKE

10 Patience is something you admire in the driver behind you and scorn in the one ahead.

—MAC MCCLEARY

11 Waiting is worse than knowing. Grief rends the heart cleanly, that it may begin to heal; waiting shreds the spirit.

—MORGAN LLYWELYN
The Wind from Hastings

12 There's a fine line between fishing and standing on the shore like an idiot.

—STEVEN WRIGHT

13 Regardless of how much patience we have, we would prefer never to use any of it.

—JAMES T. O'BRIEN

14 A man without patience is a lamp without oil.

—ANDRÉS SEGOVIA

15 Impatience can be a virtue, if you practice it on yourself.

—ROD MCKUEN
1985 Book of Days

16 He who is impatient waits twice.

—MACK MCGINNIS

17 One of the great disadvantages of hurry is that it takes such a long time.

—G. K. CHESTERTON

18 We may be willing to tell a story twice but we are never willing to hear it more than once.

—WILLIAM HAZLITT

1 How can a society that exists on instant mashed potatoes, packaged cake mixes, frozen dinners, and instant cameras teach patience to its young?

—PAUL SWEENEY

2 Patience often gets the credit that belongs to fatigue.

—FRANKLIN P. JONES

THE DIFFERENCE BETWEEN A HERO AND A COWARD . . .

3 The difference between a hero and a coward is one step sideways.

—GENE HACKMAN

4 Life shrinks or expands in proportion to one's courage.

—*The Diary of Anaïs Nin*
edited by Gunther Stuhlmann

5 Real courage is when you know you're licked before you begin, but you begin anyway and see it through no matter what.

—HARPER LEE
To Kill a Mockingbird

6 Courage is being scared to death—and saddling up anyway.

—JOHN WAYNE

7 It is often easier to fight for principles than to live up to them.

—ADLAI E. STEVENSON

8 Courage is the art of being the only one who knows you're scared to death.

—EARL WILSON

9 Facing it—always facing it—that's the way to get through. Face it!

—JOSEPH CONRAD

10 Pain nourishes courage. You can't be brave if you've only had wonderful things happen to you.

—MARY TYLER MOORE

11 Success is never final and failure never total. It's courage that counts.

—*Success Unlimited*

12 Courage is the ladder on which all the other virtues mount.

—CLARE BOOTHE LUCE

13 It's when you run away that you're most liable to stumble.

—CASEY ROBINSON

14 Curiosity will conquer fear even more than bravery will.

—JAMES STEPHENS

15 Courage is often lack of insight, whereas cowardice in many cases is based on good information.

—PETER USTINOV

16 Bravery never goes out of fashion.

—WILLIAM MAKEPEACE THACKERAY

1 There is a time to take counsel of your fears, and there is a time to never listen to any fear.
—GEN. GEORGE S. PATTON

2 Keep your fears to yourself, but share your courage.
—ROBERT LOUIS STEVENSON

3 You can't test courage cautiously.
—ANNIE DILLARD
An American Childhood

4 Courage is not the towering oak that sees storms come and go; it is the fragile blossom that opens in the snow.
—ALICE MACKENZIE SWAIM

5 Courage is contagious. When a brave man takes a stand, the spines of others are stiffened.
—REV. BILLY GRAHAM

6 The way you overcome shyness is to become so wrapped up in something that you forget to be afraid.
—LADY BIRD JOHNSON

A LITTLE KINDNESS . . .

7 A little kindness from person to person is better than a vast love for all humankind.
—RICHARD DEHMEL

8 The everyday kindness of the back roads more than makes up for the acts of greed in the headlines.
—CHARLES KURALT
On the Road With Charles Kuralt

9 A profusion of pink roses bending ragged in the rain speaks to me of all gentleness and its enduring.
—*The Collected Later Poems of William Carlos Williams*

10 Resolve to be tender with the young, compassionate with the aged, sympathetic with the striving, and tolerant with the weak and the wrong. Sometime in life you will have been all of these.
—BOB GODDARD

11 The heart is the toughest part of the body. Tenderness is in the hands.
—CAROLYN FORCHÉ
The Country Between Us

12 You cannot do a kindness too soon, for you never know how soon it will be too late.
—RALPH WALDO EMERSON

13 Life is short and we never have enough time for gladdening the hearts of those who travel the way with us. Oh, be swift to love! Make haste to be kind.
—HENRI FRÉDÉRIC AMIEL

1 There is nothing stronger in the world than gentleness.
—HAN SUYIN
A Many-Splendored Thing

2 How sweet it is when the strong are also gentle!
—LIBBIE FUDIM

3 Kindness consists in loving people more than they deserve.
—JOSEPH JOUBERT

4 Kindness is never wasted. If it has no effect on the recipient, at least it benefits the bestower.
—S. H. SIMMONS

5 Write injuries in sand, kindnesses in marble.
—FRENCH PROVERB

6 Ask any decent person what he thinks matters most in human conduct: five to one his answer will be "kindness."
—KENNETH CLARK

7 Two important things are to have a genuine interest in people and to be kind to them. Kindness, I've discovered, is everything in life.
—ISAAC BASHEVIS SINGER

8 Always try to be a little kinder than is necessary.
—JAMES M. BARRIE

9 Kindness is more important than wisdom, and the recognition of this is the beginning of wisdom.
—THEODORE ISAAC RUBIN, MD
One to One

10 When I was young, I admired clever people. Now that I am old, I admire kind people.
—ABRAHAM JOSHUA HESCHEL

11 Praise can give criticism a lead around the first turn and still win the race.
—BERN WILLIAMS
in *National Enquirer*

12 How beautiful a day can be when kindness touches it.
—GEORGE ELLISTON

13 One kind word can warm three winter months.
—JAPANESE PROVERB

14 Kind words can be short and easy to speak, but their echoes are truly endless.
—MOTHER TERESA OF CALCUTTA

15 Tenderness is passion in repose.
—JOSEPH JOUBERT

16 Kindness is a language which the deaf can hear and the blind can read.
—MARK TWAIN

1 Kindness can become its own motive. We are made kind by being kind.

—ERIC HOFFER
The Passionate State of Mind

2 A pat on the back, though only a few vertebrae removed from a kick in the pants, is miles ahead in results.

—BENNETT CERF

3 A warm smile is the universal language of kindness.

—WILLIAM ARTHUR WARD
"Reward Yourself"

4 When we put ourselves in the other person's place, we're less likely to want to put him in his place.

—*Farmer's Digest*

5 He best can pity who has felt the woe.

—JOHN GAY

6 Could a greater miracle take place than for us to look through each other's eyes for an instant?

—HENRY DAVID THOREAU

7 You never really understand a person until you consider things from his point of view.

—HARPER LEE
To Kill a Mockingbird

8 Feelings are everywhere—be gentle.

—J. MASAI

9 Never does the human soul appear so strong and noble as when it forgoes revenge and dares to forgive an injury.

—E. H. CHAPIN

10 One of the most lasting pleasures you can experience is the feeling that comes over you when you genuinely forgive an enemy— whether he knows it or not.

—O. A. BATTISTA
in *Quote Magazine*

11 A forgiveness ought to be like a canceled note, torn in two and burned up, so that it can never be shown against the man.

—HENRY WARD BEECHER

12 Forgiving and being forgiven are two names for the same thing. The important thing is that a discord has been resolved.

—C. S. LEWIS

13 He who cannot forgive others destroys the bridge over which he himself must pass.

—GEORGE HERBERT

14 When a deep injury is done us, we never recover until we forgive.

—ALAN PATON

1 Forgiveness is a gift of high value. Yet its cost is nothing.
—BETTY SMITH
A Tree Grows in Brooklyn

2 One of the secrets of a long and fruitful life is to forgive everybody everything every night before you go to bed.
—ANN LANDERS

3 Forgiveness is a funny thing. It warms the heart and cools the sting.
—WILLIAM ARTHUR WARD

4 Forgive your enemies—if you can't get back at them any other way.
—FRANKLIN P. JONES

GOODNESS IS THE ONLY INVESTMENT . . .

5 Goodness is the only investment that never fails.
—HENRY DAVID THOREAU

6 On the whole, human beings want to be good, but not too good, and not quite all the time.
—GEORGE ORWELL

7 All that is worth cherishing in this world begins in the heart, not the head.
—Quoted by SUZANNE CHAZIN in *The New York Times*

8 Ten thousand bad traits cannot make a single good one any the less good.
—ROBERT LOUIS STEVENSON

9 The line separating good and evil passes not through states, nor between political parties either—but right through every human heart.
—ALEKSANDR I. SOLZHENITSYN
The Gulag Archipelago

10 Some people strengthen the society just by being the kind of people they are.
—JOHN W. GARDNER

11 Those who bring sunshine to the lives of others cannot keep it from themselves.
—JAMES MATTHEW BARRIE

12 It's not true that nice guys finish last. Nice guys are winners before the game even starts.
—ADDISON WALKER

13 Sincerity resembles a spice. Too much repels you and too little leaves you wanting.
—BILL COPELAND

14 If you haven't any charity in your heart, you have the worst kind of heart trouble.
—BOB HOPE

1 The work of an unknown good man is like a vein of water flowing hidden underground, secretly making the ground greener.
—THOMAS CARLYLE

2 Generosity always wins favor, particularly when accompanied by modesty.
—JOHANN WOLFGANG VON GOETHE

3 People want to know how much you care before they care how much you know.
—JAMES F. HIND
in *The Wall Street Journal*

4 Goodwill is earned by many acts; it can be lost by one.
—DUNCAN STUART

GRATITUDE IS A SOMETIME THING . . .

5 Gratitude is a sometime thing in this world. Just because you've been feeding them all winter, don't expect the birds to take it easy on your grass seed.
—BILL VAUGHAN
in Kansas City *Star*

6 Gratitude is the memory of the heart.
—J. B. MASSIEU

7 Swift gratitude is the sweetest.
—GREEK PROVERB

The hardest arithmetic to master is that which enables us to count our blessings. 8
—ERIC HOFFER
Reflections On The Human Condition

Silent gratitude isn't very much use to anyone. 9
—G. B. STERN
Robert Louis Stevenson

Feeling gratitude and not expressing it is like wrapping a present and not giving it. 10
—WILLIAM ARTHUR WARD

One must be poor to know the luxury of giving. 11
—GEORGE ELIOT

To know the value of generosity, it is necessary to have suffered from the cold indifference of others. 12
—EUGENE CLOUTIER

Sometimes we need to remind ourselves that thankfulness is indeed a virtue. 13
—WILLIAM J. BENNETT
The Moral Compass

Appreciation is like an insurance policy. It has to be renewed every now and then. 14
—DAVE MCINTYRE

PERSEVERANCE IS NOT A LONG RACE . . .

1 Perseverance is not a long race;
it is many short races one after
another.

—WALTER ELLIOTT
The Spiritual Life

2 Fall seven times, stand up eight.

—JAPANESE PROVERB

3 Let me tell you the secret that has
led me to my goal. My strength
lies solely in my tenacity.

—LOUIS PASTEUR

4 Great works are performed, not
by strength, but by perseverance.

—SAMUEL JOHNSON

5 Vitality shows not only in the ability to persist but in the ability to
start over.

—F. SCOTT FITZGERALD

6 By perseverance the snail reached
the ark.

—CHARLES HADDON SPURGEON

7 In the confrontation between the
stream and the rock, the stream
always wins—not through strength
but by perseverance.

—H. JACKSON BROWN
A Father's Book of Wisdom

8 What counts is not necessarily the
size of the dog in the fight—it's
the size of the fight in the dog.

—DWIGHT D. EISENHOWER

9 A professional is someone who
can do his best work when he
doesn't feel like it.

—ALISTAIR COOKE

10 The man who removes a mountain begins by carrying away small
stones.

—CHINESE PROVERB

11 If you can find a path with no
obstacles, it probably doesn't lead
anywhere.

—FRANK A. CLARK

12 Perseverance is the hard work you
do after you get tired of doing the
hard work you already did.

—NEWT GINGRICH

13 Go the extra mile. It's never
crowded.

—*Executive Speechwriter Newsletter*

14 Lord, give me the determination
and tenacity of a weed.

—MRS. LEON R. WALTERS

FOR BETTER OR WORSE

It has been my experience that folks who have no vices have very few virtues.
—ABRAHAM LINCOLN

WE ALL KNOW A FOOL . . .

1 We all know a fool when we see
one—but not when we are one.
—ARNOLD H. GLASOW

2 It is wise to remember that you
are one of those who can be
fooled some of the time.
—LAURENCE J. PETER
Peter's Almanac

3 There is a foolish corner in the
brain of the wisest man.
—ARISTOTLE

4 You will do foolish things, but do
them with enthusiasm.
—COLETTE

5 April 1 is the day upon which we
are reminded what we are on the
other 364.
—MARK TWAIN

6 Only a fool tests the depth of the
water with both feet.
—AFRICAN PROVERB

7 Anyone can make a mistake.
A fool insists on repeating it.
—ROBERTINE MAYNARD

8 A fool judges people by the
presents they give him.
—CHINESE SAYING

9 Astrology proves one scientific
fact, and one only; there's one
born every minute.
—PATRICK MOORE

10 Only a fool argues with a skunk,
a mule or the cook.
—HARRY OLIVER
Desert Rat Scrap Book

11 The ultimate result of shielding
men from the effects of folly is
to fill the world with fools.
—HERBERT SPENCER
Essays

12 The surprising thing about young
fools is how many survive to
become old fools.
—DOUG LARSON

13 Self-delusion is pulling in your
stomach when you step on the
scales.
—PAUL SWEENEY

14 Any fool can criticize, condemn
and complain—and most do.
—DALE CARNEGIE
*How to Win Friends and Influence
People*

15 Anybody with money to burn
will easily find someone to tend
the fire.
—*Pocket Crossword Puzzles*

1 Follies change their type but foolishness remains.

—ERICH KASTNER

2 I'm not denyin' the women are foolish: God Almighty made 'em to match the men.

—GEORGE ELIOT

3 Let us be thankful for the fools. But for them the rest of us could not succeed.

—MARK TWAIN

4 Everybody has the right to express what he thinks. That, of course, lets the crackpots in. But if you cannot tell a crackpot when you see one, then you ought to be taken in.

—HARRY S. TRUMAN

5 Some people get lost in thought because it's such unfamiliar territory.

—G. BEHN

6 A fanatic is someone who can't change his mind and won't change the subject.

—WINSTON CHURCHILL

7 While intelligent people can often simplify the complex, a fool is more likely to complicate the simple.

—GERALD W. GRUMET, MD
in *Readings*

There are 40 kinds of lunacy, but only one kind of common sense. 8

—AFRICAN PROVERB

A bore is someone who persists in 9 holding his own views after we have enlightened him with ours.

—MALCOLM S. FORBES

Bores bore each other, too, but 10 it never seems to teach them anything.

—DON MARQUIS

Some people can stay longer in 11 an hour than others can in a week.

—WILLIAM DEAN HOWELLS

A healthy male adult bore con- 12 sumes each year one-and-a-half times his own weight in other people's patience.

—JOHN UPDIKE
Assorted Prose

Everyone is a bore to someone. 13 That is unimportant. The thing to avoid is being a bore to oneself.

—GERALD BRENAN

A bore is a fellow talker who can 14 change the subject to his topic of conversation faster than you can change it back to yours.

—LAURENCE J. PETER
Peter's Quotations

1 People who insist on telling their dreams are among the terrors of the breakfast table.

—MAX BEERBOHM

2 Don't approach a goat from the front, a horse from the back or a fool from any side.

—YIDDISH PROVERB

3 Human reason is like a drunken man on horseback; set it up on one side, and it tumbles over on the other.

—MARTIN LUTHER

LOST BY INDIFFERENCE . . .

4 More good things in life are lost by indifference than ever were lost by active hostility.

—ROBERT GORDON MENZIES

5 Apathy is the glove into which evil slips its hand.

—BODIE THOENE

6 Love me or hate me, but spare me your indifference.

—LIBBIE FUDIM

7 I have a very strong feeling that the opposite of love is not hate— it's apathy.

—LEO BUSCAGLIA
Love

8 It is a perplexing and unpleasant truth that when men have something worth fighting for, they do not feel like fighting.

—ERIC HOFFER
The True Believer

9 There is nothing harder than the softness of indifference.

—JUAN MONTALVO

10 The tragedy of modern man is not that he knows less and less about the meaning of his own life but that it bothers him less and less.

—VACLAV HAVEL

11 Crime expands according to our willingness to put up with it.

—BARRY FARBER

GROW ANGRY SLOWLY . . .

12 Grow angry slowly—there's plenty of time.

—RALPH WALDO EMERSON

13 Anger is a wind which blows out the lamp of the mind.

—ROBERT G. INGERSOLL

14 Anger is not only inevitable, it is necessary. Its absence means indifference, the most disastrous of all human failings.

—ARTHUR PONSONBY

1 Anger is a symptom, a way of cloaking and expressing feelings too awful to experience directly—hurt, bitterness, grief and, most of all, fear.

—JOAN RIVERS
Still Talking

2 Getting angry can sometimes be like leaping into a wonderfully responsive sports car, gunning the motor, taking off at high speed and then discovering the brakes are out of order.

—MAGGIE SCARF
in *The New York Times Magazine*

3 Anyone can become angry. That is easy. But to be angry with the right person, to the right degree, at the right time, for the right purpose and in the right way—that is not easy.

—ARISTOTLE

4 Anger is a bad counselor.

—FRENCH PROVERB

5 Resentment is an extremely bitter diet, and eventually poisonous. I have no desire to make my own toxins.

—NEIL KINNOCK

6 There's a bit of ancient wisdom that appeals to us: it's a saying that a fight starts only with the second blow.

—HUGH ALLEN

7 I will permit no man to narrow and degrade my soul by making me hate him.

—BOOKER T. WASHINGTON

8 My life is in the hands of any fool who makes me lose my temper.

—JOSEPH HUNTER

9 It is only our bad temper that we put down to being tired or worried or hungry; we put our good temper down to ourselves.

—C. S. LEWIS
Mere Christianity

10 Temper, if ungoverned, governs the whole man.

—ANTHONY SHAFTESBURY

11 Temper is a quality that at a critical moment brings out the best in steel and the worst in people.

—WILLIAM P. GROHSE

12 Revenge has no more quenching effect on emotions than salt water has on thirst.

—WALTER WECKLER

13 Violence is the last refuge of the incompetent.

—ISAAC ASIMOV

14 A man that studieth revenge keeps his own wounds green.

—FRANCIS BACON

1 Getting even throws everything out of balance.

—JOE BROWNE
in Post-Gazette
(Pittsburgh, Pennsylvania)

2 If a small thing has the power to make you angry, does that not indicate something about your size?

—SYDNEY J. HARRIS

3 I imagine one of the reasons people cling to their hates so stubbornly is because they sense, once hate is gone, they will be forced to deal with pain.

—JAMES BALDWIN

4 To carry a grudge is like being stung to death by one bee.

—WILLIAM H. WALTON

5 Nothing lowers the level of conversation more than raising the voice.

—STANLEY HOROWITZ

6 Not the fastest horse can catch a word spoken in anger.

—CHINESE PROVERB

7 Speak when you are angry and you will make the best speech you will ever regret.

—AMBROSE BIERCE

8 Hot words make a real cool friendship.

—FLO ASHWORTH
in Advertiser & News (Dawsonville, Georgia)

9 The best remedy for a short temper is a long walk.

—JACQUELINE SCHIFF
in National Enquirer

GOSSIP NEEDN'T BE FALSE . . .

10 Gossip needn't be false to be evil—there's a lot of truth that shouldn't be passed around.

—FRANK A. CLARK

11 There is nothing busier than an idle rumor.

—HERBERT V. PROCHNOW
The New Speaker's Treasury of Wit and Wisdom

12 In our appetite for gossip, we tend to gobble down everything before us, only to find, too late, that it is our ideals we have consumed, and we have not been enlarged by the feasts but only diminished.

—PICO IYER
in Time

13 Knowledge is power, if you know it about the right person.

—ETHEL WATTS

1 A gossip is a person who creates the smoke in which other people assume there's fire.
—DAN BENNETT

2 Gossip is that which no one claims to like—but everybody enjoys.
—JOSEPH CONRAD

3 Bad news goes about in clogs, good news in stockinged feet.
—WELSH PROVERB

4 The gossip of the future may not be a backbiting, nosy, tongue-wagging two-face but a super-megabyte, random-access, digital interface.
—RONALD B. ZEH

5 Some people will believe anything if it is whispered to them.
—PIERRE DE MARIVAUX

6 Men gossip less than women, but mean it.
—MIGNON MCLAUGHLIN

7 Scandal is the coin of contemporary celebrity. It keeps the public interested.
—RICHARD CORLISS

8 He who is caught in a lie is not believed when he tells the truth.
—SPANISH PROVERB

9 Gossip, unlike river water, flows both ways.
—MICHAEL KORDA

10 Trying to squash a rumor is like trying to unring a bell.
—SHANA ALEXANDER

11 A rumor without a leg to stand on will get around some other way.
—JOHN TUDOR
in *Omni*

12 Just because a rumor is idle doesn't mean it isn't working.
—MAURICE SEITTER

13 To speak ill of others is a dishonest way of praising ourselves.
—WILL DURANT

WHEN FLATTERERS MEET . . .

14 When flatterers meet, the devil goes to dinner.
—ENGLISH PROVERB

15 Of all music, that which most pleases the ear is applause. But it has no score. It ends and is carried off by the wind. Nothing remains.
—ENRIQUE SOLARI

16 Flattery is counterfeit money which, but for vanity, would have no circulation.
—FRANÇOIS DE LA ROCHEFOUCAULD

17 Beware the flatterer: he feeds you with an empty spoon.
—COSINO DEGREGRIO

1 A detour is a straight road which turns on the charm.

—ALBERT BRIE
Le Devoir

2 Flatterers look like friends, as wolves like dogs.

—GEORGE CHAPMAN

3 The punishment for vanity is flattery.

—WILHELM RAABE

4 We protest against unjust criticism, but we accept unearned applause.

—JOSÉ NAROSKY
Si Todos Los Sueños

5 I have yet to be bored by someone paying me a compliment.

—OTTO VAN ISCH

6 Flattery is all right—if you don't inhale.

—ADLAI E. STEVENSON

7 Praise, if you don't swallow it, can't hurt you.

—MORT WALKER

8 Praise can be your most valuable asset as long as you don't aim it at yourself.

—O. A. BATTISTA

9 Fish for no compliments; they are generally caught in shallow water.

—D. SMITH

10 Praise is warming and desirable. But it is an earned thing. It has to be deserved, like a hug from a child.

—PHYLLIS McGINLEY
in *The Saturday Evening Post*

11 Sometimes we deny being worthy of praise, hoping to generate an argument we would be pleased to lose.

—CULLEN HIGHTOWER

12 He who praises everybody praises nobody.

—SAMUEL JOHNSON

FORBIDDEN FRUIT . . .

13 While forbidden fruit is said to taste sweeter, it usually spoils faster.

—ABIGAIL VAN BUREN

14 A compulsion is a highbrow term for a temptation we're not trying too hard to resist.

—HUGH ALLEN

15 Most people want to be delivered from temptation but would like it to keep in touch.

—ROBERT ORBEN

16 Those who flee temptation generally leave a forwarding address.

—LANE OLINGHOUSE

1 Temptation usually comes in through a door that has deliberately been left open.

—Arnold H. Glasow

2 Temptations, unlike opportunities, will always give you many second chances.

—O. A. Battista

3 There is no original sin; it has all been done before.

—Louis Dudek

4 Be cautious. Opportunity does the knocking for temptation too.

—Al Batt

5 Being virtuous is no feat once temptation ceases.

—Danish proverb

6 Nothing makes it easier to resist temptation than a proper bringing-up, a sound set of values—and witnesses.

—Franklin P. Jones

7 In this era of rapid change, one thing remains constant: it's easier to pray for forgiveness than to resist temptation.

—Sol Kendon

8 About the only time losing is more fun than winning is when you're fighting temptation.

—Tom Wilson

9 Come good times or bad, there is always a market for things nobody needs.

—Kin Hubbard

10 When there's a lot of it around, you never want it very much.

—Peg Bracken
The I Hate to Cook Almanack

LAZINESS HAS MANY DISGUISES . . .

11 Laziness has many disguises. Soon "winter doldrums" will become "spring fever."

—Bern Williams
in *National Enquirer*

12 He who is carried on another's back does not appreciate how far off the town is.

—African proverb

13 If you get a reputation as an early riser, you can sleep till noon.

—Irish proverb

14 Cultivate the habit of early rising. It is unwise to keep the head long on a level with the feet.

—Henry David Thoreau

15 Laziness may appear attractive, but work gives satisfaction.

—Anne Frank
The Diary of a Young Girl

1 The safest road to hell is the gradual one—the gentle slope, soft underfoot, without sudden turnings, without milestones, without signposts.

—C. S. Lewis
The Screwtape Letters

2 Laziness is nothing more than resting before you get tired.

—Jules Renard

3 A lot of what passes for depression these days is nothing more than a body saying that it needs work.

—Geoffrey Norman

4 Beware of the man who won't be bothered with details.

—William Feather Sr.

5 It is better to have loafed and lost than never to have loafed at all.

—James Thurber

6 The day will happen whether or not you get up.

—John Ciardi

7 I'm lazy. But it's the lazy people who invented the wheel and the bicycle because they didn't like walking or carrying things.

—Lech Walesa

8 About the only thing that comes to us without effort is old age.

—Gloria Pitzer

9 I can do only one thing at a time, but I can avoid doing many things simultaneously.

—Ashleigh Brilliant

10 What a fearful object a long-neglected duty gets to be!

—Chauncey Wright

11 A life of ease is a difficult pursuit.

—William Cowper

12 Most of our so-called reasoning consists in finding arguments for going on believing as we already do.

—James Harvey Robinson
The Mind in the Making

13 No one ever excused his way to success.

—Dave Del Dotto
How to Make Nothing But Money

14 Excuses are the nails used to build a house of failure.

—Don Wilder and Bill Rechin

15 Whoever wants to be a judge of human nature should study people's excuses.

— Friedrich Hebbel

16 Don't tell me how hard you work. Tell me how much you get done.

—James Ling
in *Newsweek*

1 To be idle requires a strong sense of personal identity.
—Robert Louis Stevenson

2 There are no shortcuts to any place worth going.
—Beverly Sills

3 The older generation thought nothing of getting up at five every morning—and the younger generation doesn't think much of it either.
—John J. Welsh

THE FAULTS OF OTHERS . . .

4 Rare is the person who can weigh the faults of others without putting his thumb on the scales.
—Byron J. Langenfield

5 Only God is in a position to look down on anyone.
—Sarah Brown

6 The unforgiving man assumes a judgment that not even the theologians has [sic] given to God.
—Sydney J. Harris

7 I have never for one instant seen clearly within myself. How then would you have me judge the deeds of others?
—Maurice Maeterlinck

8 Moral indignation is jealousy with a halo.
—H. G. Wells

9 Other people's faults are like bees — if we don't see them, they don't harm us.
—Luis Vigil
Pensamientos y Observaciónes

10 Make no judgments where you have no compassion.
—Anne McCaffrey
Dragonquest

11 How much easier it is to be critical than to be correct.
—Benjamin Disraeli

12 What we all tend to complain about most in other people are those things we don't like about ourselves.
—William Wharton
Tidings

13 I don't like a man to be efficient. He's likely to be not human enough.
—Felix Frankfruter

14 When a man points a finger at someone else, he should remember that three of his fingers are pointing at himself.
—Anonymous

15 Ought is not a word we use to other people. It is a word we should reserve for ourselves.
—Sister Wendy Beckett

1 Perhaps no phenomenon contains so much destructive feeling as "moral indignation," which permits envy or hate to be acted out under the guise of virtue.

—ERICH FROMM

2 If you judge people, you have no time to love them.

—MOTHER TERESA OF CALCUTTA

3 Speak not against anyone whose burden you have not weighed yourself.

—MARION BRADLEY
Black Trillium

4 Puritanism is the haunting fear that someone, somewhere, may be happy.

—H. L. MENCKEN

5 This is a do-it-yourself test for paranoia: you know you've got it when you can't think of anything that's your fault.

—ROBERT M. HUTCHINS

6 That which we call sin in others is experiment for us.

—RALPH WALDO EMERSON

7 We all have weaknesses. But I have figured that others have put up with mine so tolerantly that I would be less than fair not to make a reasonable discount for theirs.

—WILLIAM ALLEN WHITE

8 We are all inclined to judge ourselves by our ideals; others, by their acts.

—HAROLD NICOLSON

9 Distrust all in whom the impulse to punish is powerful.

—FRIEDRICH NIETZSCHE

10 Nothing so needs reforming as other people's habits.

—MARK TWAIN

11 Our faults irritate us most when we see them in others.

—PENNSYLVANIA DUTCH PROVERB

12 The enthusiastic, to those who are not, are always something of a trial.

—ALBAN GOODIER

13 There is little room left for wisdom when one is full of judgment.

—MALCOLM HEIN

14 Nothing in the world is so rare as a person one can always put up with.

—GIACOMO LEOPARDI

15 When nobody around you seems to measure up, it's time to check your yardstick.

—BILL LEMLEY

1 It has been my experience that folks who have no vices have very few virtues.

—ABRAHAM LINCOLN

2 There are certain small faults that offset great virtues. There are certain great faults that are forgotten in small virtues.

—GRANTLAND RICE WATTS

3 Accept me as I am—only then will we discover each other.

—FROM FEDERICO FELLINI'S *8 1/2*

4 The less secure a man is, the more likely he is to have extreme prejudices.

—CLINT EASTWOOD

5 Nothing dies so hard, or rallies so often, as intolerance.

—HENRY WARD BEECHER

6 Prejudices are the chains forged by ignorance to keep men apart.

—COUNTESS OF BLESSINGTON

7 Prejudice is a disease characterized by hardening of the categories.

—WILLIAM ARTHUR

8 A prejudice is a vagrant opinion without visible means of support.

—AMBROSE BIERCE

9 It is never too late to give up our prejudices.

—HENRY DAVID THOREAU

10 Every bigot was once a child free of prejudice.

—SISTER MARY DE LOURDES

11 Too many of our prejudices are like pyramids upside down. They rest on tiny, trivial incidents, but they spread upward and outward until they fill our minds.

—WILLIAM McCHESNEY MARTIN

STUPIDITY WON'T KILL YOU . . .

12 Stupidity won't kill you, but it can make you sweat.

—ENGLISH PROVERB

13 Ignorance is not bliss—it is oblivion.

—PHILIP WYLIE

14 I am patient with stupidity but not with those who are proud of it.

—EDITH SITWELL

15 The greatest obstacle to discovering the shape of the earth, the continents and the ocean was not ignorance but the illusion of knowledge.

—DANIEL J. BOORSTIN
The Discoverers

16 Ignorance is bold, and knowledge reserved.

—THUCYDIDES

1 The trouble with most folks isn't so much their ignorance, as knowing so many things that ain't so.
—JOSH BILLINGS

2 Sometimes the best way to convince someone he is wrong is to let him have his way.
—RED O'DONNELL

3 Everybody is ignorant, only on different subjects.
—WILL ROGERS

4 Nothing will divide this nation more than ignorance, and nothing can bring us together better than an educated population.
—JOHN SCULLEY
in *The Atlantic*

5 Preconceived notions are the locks on the door to wisdom.
—MERRY BROWNE
in *National Enquirer*

6 Fears are educated into us and can, if we wish, be educated out.
—KARL A. MENNINGER, MD
The Human Mind

7 The intelligent man who is proud of his intelligence is like the condemned man who is proud of his large cell.
—SIMONE WEIL

IF MALICE OR ENVY WERE TANGIBLE . . .

8 It is never wise to seek or wish for another's misfortune. If malice or envy were tangible and had a shape, it would be the shape of a boomerang.
—CHARLEY REESE

9 Spite is never lonely; envy always tags along.
—MIGNON MCLAUGHLIN

10 Envy is the art of counting the other fellow's blessings instead of your own.
—HAROLD COFFIN

11 Do not believe those persons who say they have never been jealous. What they mean is that they have never been in love.
—GERALD BRENAN

12 Love looks through a telescope; envy, through a microscope.
—JOSH BILLINGS

13 Jealousy is all the fun you think they had.
—ERICA JONG

14 I'd never try to learn from someone I didn't envy at least a little. If I never envied, I'd never learn.
—BETSY COHEN
The Snow White Syndrome

THE CHAINS OF HABIT . . .

1 The chains of habit are generally too small to be felt until they are too strong to be broken.
—SAMUEL JOHNSON

2 Good habits are as easy to form as bad ones.
—TIM MCCARVER

3 Habits are first cobwebs, then cables.
—SPANISH PROVERB

4 Comfort comes as a guest, lingers to become a host and stays to enslave us.
—LEE S. BICKMORE

5 Habit is habit, and not to be flung out of the window by any man, but coaxed downstairs a step at a time.
—MARK TWAIN

6 A habit is a shirt made of iron.
—HAROLD HELFER

7 Habits are like supervisors that you don't notice.
—HANNES MESSEMER

8 We can often endure an extra pound of pain far more easily than we can suffer the withdrawal of an ounce of accustomed pleasure.
—SYDNEY J. HARRIS

9 Habit, if not resisted, soon becomes necessity.
—ST. AUGUSTINE

10 It is easy to assume a habit; but when you try to cast it off, it will take skin and all.
—JOSH BILLINGS

11 A habit is something you can do without thinking—which is why most of us have so many of them.
—FRANK A. CLARK

12 The best way to break a habit is to drop it.
—LEO AIKMAN

13 A bad habit never disappears miraculously; it's an undo-it-yourself project.
—ABIGAIL VAN BUREN

NEVER BE HAUGHTY . . .

14 Never be haughty to the humble. Never be humble to the haughty.
—JEFFERSON DAVIS

15 None are so empty as those who are full of themselves.
—BENJAMIN WHICHCOTE

16 The louder he talked of his honor, the faster we counted our spoons.
—RALPH WALDO EMERSON

1 He who truly knows has no
occasion to shout.
—LEONARDO DA VINCI

2 The question we do not see when
we are young is whether we own
pride or are owned by it.
—JOSEPHINE JOHNSON
The Dark Traveler

3 If you are all wrapped up in
yourself, you are overdressed.
—*The Wedded Unmother*

4 A man wrapped up in himself
makes a very small parcel.
—"Thought for the Day," BBC Radio

5 When someone sings his own
praises, he always gets the tune
too high.
—MARY H. WALDRIP

6 Vanity is the result of a delusion
that someone is paying attention.
—PAUL E. SWEENEY

7 Oh, for a pin that would puncture
pretension!
—ISAAC ASIMOV
Buy Jupiter and Other Stories

8 Men often mistake notoriety for
fame, and would rather be
remarked for their vices and follies than not be noticed at all.
—HARRY S. TRUMAN

9 It is far more impressive when
others discover your good
qualities without your help.
—JUDITH S. MARTIN

10 A modest man is usually admired—
if people ever hear of him.
—ED HOWE

11 Lord, where we are wrong,
make us willing to change; where
we are right, make us easy to
live with.
—REV. PETER MARSHALL

12 The nice thing about egotists is
that they don't talk about other
people.
—LUCILLE S. HARPER

13 The egotist always hurts the one
he loves—himself.
—BERNICE PEERS

14 The only cure for vanity is laughter. And the only fault that's
laughable is vanity.
—HENRI BERGSON

15 Pride makes some men ridiculous
but prevents others from
becoming so.
—CHARLES CALEB COLTON

16 Too great a sense of identity
makes a man feel he can do no
wrong. And too little does the
same.
—DJUNA BARNES

WHEN WE ACT

Life is a great big canvas, and you should throw all the paint on it you can.

—Danny Kaye

THE VERY ESSENCE OF LEADERSHIP . . .

1 The very essence of leadership is that you have to have a vision. You can't blow an uncertain trumpet.

—THEODORE HESBURGH

2 High sentiments always win in the end. The leaders who offer blood, toil, tears and sweat always get more out of their followers than those who offer safety and a good time. When it comes to the pinch, human beings are heroic.

—George Orwell
Collected Essays, Journalism and Letters

3 Consensus is the negation of leadership.

—MARGARET THATCHER

4 You do not lead by hitting people over the head. That's assault, not leadership.

—DWIGHT D. EISENHOWER

5 Lots of folks confuse bad management with destiny.

—KIN HUBBARD

6 Never tell people how to do things. Tell them what to do and they will surprise you with their ingenuity.

—GEN. GEORGE S. PATTON JR.

7 Rules are made for people who aren't willing to make up their own.

—CHUCK YEAGER AND CHARLES LEERHSEN
Press On!

8 A leader knows what's best to do; a manager knows merely how best to do it.

—KEN ADELMAN

9 Leadership is a potent combination of strategy and character. But if you must be without one, be without the strategy.

—GEN. H. NORMAN SCHWARZKOPF

10 A leader who keeps his ear to the ground allows his rear end to become a target.

—ANGIE PAPADAKIS

11 One measure of leadership is the caliber of people who choose to follow you.

—DENNIS A. PEER

12 The person who knows how will always have a job. But the person who knows why will be his boss.

—CARL C. WOOD

13 Anyone can hold the helm when the sea is calm.

—PUBLILIUS SYRUS

14 Nothing great was ever achieved without enthusiasm.

—RALPH WALDO EMERSON

1 Knowledge cannot make us all leaders, but it can help us decide which leader to follow.
—*Management Digest*

2 Wise are those who learn that the bottom line doesn't always have to be their top priority.
—WILLIAM ARTHUR WARD

3 The mark of a true professional is giving more than you get.
—ROBERT KIRBY

4 Rank does not confer privilege or give power. It imposes responsibility.
—PETER DRUCKER
in *Fortune*

5 A man who enjoys responsibility usually gets it. A man who merely likes exercising authority usually loses it.
—MALCOLM S. FORBES

6 Few things are harder to put up with than the annoyance of a good example.
—MARK TWAIN

7 He that would be a leader must be a bridge.
—WELSH PROVERB

8 Life is like a dog-sled team. If you ain't the lead dog, the scenery never changes.
—LEWIS GRIZZARD

9 The speed of the leader determines the rate of the pack.
—WAYNE LUKAS

10 If you want truly to understand something, try to change it.
—KURT LEWIN

11 We still think of a powerful man as a born leader and a powerful woman as an anomaly.
—MARGARET ATWOOD

12 Asking "Who ought to be boss?" is like asking "Who ought to be the tenor in the quartet?" Obviously, the man who can sing tenor.
—HENRY FORD

13 A great leader is the one who can show people that their self-interest is different from that which they perceived.
—BARNEY FRANK

14 No person can be a great leader unless he takes genuine joy in the successes of those under him.
—W. A. NANCE

15 First-rate men hire first-rate men; second-rate men hire third-rate men.
—LEO ROSTEN

16 It's easy to make a buck. It's a lot tougher to make a difference.
—TOM BROKAW

1 The things we fear most in organi-
zations—fluctuations, disturbances,
imbalances—are the primary
sources of creativity.
—MARGARET J. WHEATLEY
Leadership and the New Science

2 Change starts when someone sees
the next step.
—WILLIAM DRAYTON
in *Esquire*

3 I am more afraid of an army of
100 sheep led by a lion than an
army of 100 lions led by a sheep.
—TALLEYRAND

4 It's better to be a lion for a day
than a sheep all your life.
—SISTER KENNY

WHAT GREAT THING WOULD
YOU ATTEMPT . . .

5 What great thing would you
attempt if you knew you could
not fail?
—ROBERT H. SCHULLER

6 Why not upset the apple cart?
If you don't, the apples will rot
anyway.
—FRANK A. CLARK

7 Determine that the thing can and
shall be done, and then we shall
find the way.
—ABRAHAM LINCOLN

8 When a man's willing and eager,
the gods join in.
—AESCHYLUS

9 Trust in God and do something.
—MARY LYON

10 Action may not always be happiness, but there is no happiness
without action.
—BENJAMIN DISRAELI

11 There is a close correlation
between getting up in the morning and getting up in the world.
—RON DENTINGER
in *Chronicle* (Dodgerville, Wisconsin)

12 Noble deeds and hot baths are the
best cures for depression.
—DODIE SMITH
I Capture The Castle

13 My view is that to sit back and let
fate play its hand out and never
influence it is not the way man
was meant to operate.
—JOHN GLENN

14 People judge you by your actions,
not your intentions. You may have
a heart of gold, but so has a hard-
boiled egg.
—*Good Reading*

15 Let him that would move the
world, first move himself.
—SOCRATES

1 All glory comes from daring to begin.
—EUGENE F. WARE

2 Everything comes to he who hustles while he waits.
—THOMAS A. EDISON

3 Well done is better than well said.
—BENJAMIN FRANKLIN

4 You can't build a reputation on what you are going to do.
—HENRY FORD

5 In life, as in a football game, the principle to follow is: hit the line hard.
—THEODORE ROOSEVELT

6 If you never budge, don't expect a push.
—MALCOLM S. FORBES

7 You must get involved to have an impact. No one is impressed with the won-lost record of the referee.
—JOHN H. HOLCOMB
The Militant Moderate

8 Swing hard, in case they throw the ball where you're swinging.
—DUKE SNIDER

9 Life is a great big canvas, and you should throw all the paint on it you can.
—DANNY KAYE

10 Success is a ladder that cannot be climbed with your hands in your pockets.
—AMERICAN PROVERB

11 Few wishes come true by themselves.
—JUNE SMITH
in *Sentinel* (Orlando, Florida)

12 Dig the well before you are thirsty.
—CHINESE PROVERB

13 Have you considered that if you "don't make waves," nobody, including yourself, will know that you are alive?
—THEODORE ISAAC RUBIN, MD

14 Many a man with no family tree has succeeded because he branched out for himself.
—LEO AIKMAN

15 God gives every bird his worm, but he does not throw it into the nest.
—SWEDISH PROVERB

16 Ask God's blessing on your work, but don't ask him to do it for you.
—DAME FLORA ROBSON
on *Friends*, BBC

17 It is easy to sit up and take notice. What is difficult is getting up and taking action.
—AL BATT

1 Not everything that is faced can be changed. But nothing can be changed until it is faced.

—JAMES BALDWIN

2 Our dilemma is that we hate change and love it at the same time; what we really want is for things to remain the same but get better.

—SYDNEY J. HARRIS

3 Just as iron rusts from disuse, even so does inaction spoil the intellect.

—LEONARDO DA VINCI

4 Men may doubt what you say, but they will believe what you do.

—LEWIS CASS

5 If your ship doesn't come in, swim out to it!

—JONATHAN WINTERS

6 Sow an act, and you reap a habit. Sow a habit, and you reap a character. Sow a character, and you reap a destiny.

—CHARLES READE

BE BOLD IN WHAT YOU STAND FOR . . .

7 Be bold in what you stand for and careful what you fall for.

—RUTH BOORSTIN
in *The Wall Street Journal*

8 Don't believe that winning is really everything. It's more important to stand for something. If you don't stand for something, what do you win?

—LANE KIRKLAND

9 Never give in—in nothing, great or small, large or petty—except to convictions of honor and good sense.

—WINSTON CHURCHILL

10 The quality of a man's life is in direct proportion to his commitment to excellence, regardless of his chosen field of endeavor.

—VINCE LOMBARDI

11 A good resolution is like an old horse which is often saddled but rarely ridden.

—MEXICAN PROVERB

12 Compromise makes a good umbrella, but a poor roof.

—JAMES RUSSELL LOWELL

13 A thing moderately good is not so good as it ought to be. Moderation in temper is always a virtue; but moderation in principle is always a vice.

—THOMAS PAINE

14 He that always gives way to others will end in having no principles of his own.

—AESOP

1 Middleness is the very enemy of
the bold.
—CHARLES KRAUTHAMMER

2 You've got to stand for somethin'
or you're gonna fall for anything.
—JOHN COUGAR MELLENCAMP
"You've Got to Stand for Somethin'"

3 Learn to say no. It will be of more
use to you than to be able to read
Latin.
—CHARLES HADDON SPURGEON

4 One-half the troubles of this life
can be traced to saying yes too
quickly and not saying no soon
enough.
—JOSH BILLINGS

5 It's important that people should
know what you stand for. It's
equally important that they know
what you won't stand for.
—MARY H. WALDRIP

6 Standing in the middle of the road
is very dangerous; you get
knocked down by the traffic from
both sides.
—MARGARET THATCHER

7 The main discomfort in being a
middle-of-the-roader is that you
get sideswiped by partisans going
in both directions.
—SYDNEY J. HARRIS

The most prominent place in hell 8
is reserved for those who are neu-
tral on the great issues of life.
—REV. BILLY GRAHAM

Never "for the sake of peace and 9
quiet" deny your own experience
or convictions.
—DAG HAMMARSKJOLD

When something important is 10
going on, silence is a lie.
—A. M. ROSENTHAL
in *The New York Times*

Please all and you please none. 11
—AESOP

He who turns the other cheek too 12
far gets it in the neck.
—H. HERT

You can lean over backward so 13
far that you fall flat on your face.
—BEN H. BAGDIKIAN

In the end it will not matter to us 14
whether we fought with flails or
reeds. It will matter to us greatly
on what side we fought.
—G. K. CHESTERTON

A man's judgment is best when he 15
can forget himself and any reputation he may have acquired and
can concentrate wholly on making
the right decisions.
—ADM. RAYMOND A. SPRUANCE

OPPORTUNITIES ARE NEVER LOST . . .

1 Opportunities are never lost. The other fellow takes those you miss.

—ANONYMOUS

2 Not many sounds in life, and I include all urban and all rural sounds, exceed in interest a knock at the door.

—CHARLES LAMB

3 The world is before you, and you need not take it or leave it as it was when you came in.

—JAMES BALDWIN

4 Opportunity is often difficult to recognize; we usually expect it to beckon us with beepers and billboards.

—WILLIAM ARTHUR WARD

5 If opportunity doesn't knock, build a door.

—MILTON BERLE

6 It is often hard to distinguish between the hard knocks in life and those of opportunity.

—FREDERICK PHILLIPS

7 Life is always walking up to us and saying, "Come on in, the living's fine," and what do we do? Back off and take its picture.

—RUSSELL BAKER

8 Opportunity is sometimes hard to recognize if you're only looking for a lucky break.

—MONTA CRANE

9 Opportunity's favorite disguise is trouble.

—FRANK TYGER
in Rotary "Scandal Sheet" (Graham, Texas)

10 Opportunities are often things you haven't noticed the first time around.

—CATHERINE DENEUVE

11 Wherever we look upon this earth, the opportunities take shape within the problems.

—NELSON A. ROCKEFELLER

12 If a window of opportunity appears, don't pull down the shade.

—TOM PETERS
The Pursuit of Wow!

13 A problem is a chance for you to do your best.

—DUKE ELLINGTON

14 Jumping at several small opportunities may get us there more quickly than waiting for one big one to come along.

—HUGH ALLEN

1 Problems are only opportunities with thorns on them.

—HUGH MILLER
Snow on the Wind

2 Opportunity is a bird that never perches.

—CLAUDE MCDONALD

3 One of the secrets of life is to make stepping stones out of stumbling blocks.

—JACK PENN

4 Today's opportunities erase yesterday's failures.

—GENE BROWN
in *News-Times* (Danbury, Connecticut)

5 I make the most of all that comes and the least of all that goes.

—SARA TEASDALE
"The Philosopher," in *Poems That Touch the Heart*, edited by A. L. Alexander

OUT ON A LIMB . . .

6 Why not go out on a limb? Isn't that where the fruit is?

—FRANK SCULLY

7 All growth, including political growth, is the result of risk-taking.

—JUDE WANNISKI

8 What isn't tried won't work.

—CLAUDE MCDONALD
in *The Christian Word*

9 What is more mortifying than to feel that you have missed the plum for want of courage to shake the tree?

—LOGAN PEARSALL SMITH

10 It is not because things are difficult that we do not dare; it is because we do not dare that they are difficult.

—SENECA

11 What would life be if we had no courage to attempt anything?

—VINCENT VAN GOGH

12 A coward meets his fate in his own hideout.

—JORGE SALVADOR LARA
El Comercio

13 All serious daring starts from within.

—EUDORA WELTY
One Writer's Beginnings

14 If you risk nothing, then you risk everything.

—GEENA DAVIS

15 Worry is like a rocking chair. It will give you something to do, but it won't get you anywhere.

—*The United Church Observer*

16 Progress always involves risks. You can't steal second base and keep your foot on first.

—FREDERICK B. WILCOX

1 Yes, risk-taking is inherently fail-
ure-prone. Otherwise, it would
be called sure-thing-taking.
—Tim McMahon

2 Take a chance! All life is a chance.
The man who goes furthest is
generally the one who is willing
to do and dare.
—*Dale Carnegie's Scrapbook*, edited by
Dorothy Carnegie

3 People wish to learn to swim and
at the same time to keep one foot
on the ground.
—Marcel Proust
Remembrance of Things Past

4 High expectations are the key to
everything.
—Sam Walton

5 If you're never scared or embar-
rassed or hurt, it means you never
take any chances.
—Julia Sorel

6 When you're skating on thin ice,
you may as well tap-dance.
—Bryce Courtenay

7 It's better to plunge into the
unknown than to try to make sure
of everything.
—Gerald Lescarbeault

8 Take calculated risks. That is quite
different from being rash.
—Gen. George S. Patton Jr.

We cannot become what we need 9
to be by remaining what we are.
—Max De Pree
Leadership Is an Art

When you reach for the stars, you 10
may not quite get one, but you
won't come up with a handful of
mud either.
—Leo Burnett

In skating over thin ice, our safety 11
is in our speed.
—Ralph Waldo Emerson

You are permitted in time of great 12
danger to walk with the devil until
you have crossed the bridge.
—Bulgarian proverb

If you don't place your foot on 13
the rope, you'll never cross the
chasm.
—Liz Smith

Necessity is the mother of taking 14
chances.
—Mark Twain

If necessity is the mother of 15
invention, discontent is the father
of progress.
—David Rockefeller

Sometimes the fool who rushes in 16
gets the job done.
—Al Bernstein

1 A man sits as many risks as he runs.
—Henry David Thoreau

2 A ship in harbor is safe—but that is not what ships are for.
—John A. Shedd

A ROAD TWICE TRAVELED . . .

3 A road twice traveled is never as long.
—Rosalie Graham

4 The meaning of life cannot be told; it has to happen to a person.
—Ira Progoff
The Symbolic & the Real

5 The winds and waves are always on the side of the ablest navigators.
—Edward Gibbon

6 The person who has had a bull by the tail once has learned 60 or 70 times as much as a person who hasn't.
—Mark Twain

7 The work will teach you how to do it.
—Estonian proverb

8 Sometimes you earn more doing the jobs that pay nothing.
—Todd Ruthman

9 When you fall in a river, you're no longer a fisherman; you're a swimmer.
—Gene Hill
in *Field & Stream*

10 Believe one who has tried it.
—Virgil

11 Information's pretty thin stuff unless mixed with experience.
—Clarence Day
The Crow's Nest

12 Only the wearer knows where the shoe pinches.
—Proverb

13 A man begins cutting his wisdom teeth the first time he bites off more than he can chew.
—Herb Caen

14 The value of experience is not in seeing much, but in seeing wisely.
—Sir William Osler

15 One thing about experience is that when you don't have very much you're apt to get a lot.
—Franklin P. Jones
in *Quote*

16 Experience is a wonderful thing; it enables you to recognize a mistake every time you repeat it.
—The Associated Press

1 We learn to walk by stumbling.
—BULGARIAN PROVERB

2 I have never let my schooling interfere with my education.
—MARK TWAIN

3 People learn something every day, and a lot of times it's that what they learned the day before was wrong.
—BILL VAUGHAN

4 Just when you think you've graduated from the school of experience, someone thinks up a new course.
—MARY H. WALDRIP

5 Experience is what you get when you don't get what you want.
—DAN STANFORD

6 Anybody who profits from the experience of others probably writes biographies.
—FRANKLIN P. JONES

7 If we could sell our experiences for what they cost us, we'd all be millionaires.
—ABIGAIL VAN BUREN

8 Half, maybe more, of the delight of experiencing is to know what you are experiencing.
—JESSAMYN WEST
Hide and Seek

Perhaps the angels who fear to tread where fools rush in used to be fools who rushed in.
—FRANKLIN P. JONES
9

HE WHO HESITATES . . .

He who hesitates is last.
—*The Wit and Wisdom of Mae West* edited by Joseph Weintraub
10

He who hesitates is sometimes saved.
—JAMES THURBER
Fables for Our Time
11

These things are good in little measure and evil in large: yeast, salt and hesitation.
—*THE TALMUD*
12

The man who insists upon seeing with perfect clearness before he decides, never decides.
—HENRI FRÉDÉRIC AMIEL
13

A man would do nothing if he waited until he could do it so well that no one could find fault.
—JOHN HENRY CARDINAL NEWMAN
14

It's better to be boldly decisive and risk being wrong than to agonize at length and be right too late.
—MARILYN MOATS KENNEDY
Across the Board
15

1 If all difficulties were known at the outset of a long journey, most of us would never start out at all.
—Dan Rather with Peter Wyden
I Remember

2 Decision is a sharp knife that cuts clean and straight. Indecision is a dull one that hacks and tears and leaves ragged edges behind.
—Jan McKeithen

3 The chief danger in life is that you may take too many precautions.
—Alfred Adler

4 You have to be careful about being too careful.
—Beryl Pfizer

5 If you wait, all that happens is that you get older.
—Larry McMurtry
Some Can Whistle

6 If you take too long in deciding what to do with your life, you'll find you've done it.
—Pam Shaw

7 To think too long about doing a thing often becomes its undoing.
—Eva Young

8 When you have to make a choice and don't make it, that is in itself a choice.
—William James

9 Half the failures in life arise from pulling in one's horse as he is leaping.
—Julius Charles Hare and Augustus William Hare

10 Give me the benefit of your convictions, if you have any; but keep your doubts to yourself, for I have enough of my own.
—Johann Wolfgang von Goethe

11 Throughout history, the most common debilitating human ailment has been cold feet.
—*Country*

12 Calculation never made a hero.
—John Henry Cardinal Newman

13 He who hesitates is interrupted.
—Franklin P. Jones

If You Can't Make a Mistake . . .

14 If you can't make a mistake, you can't make anything.
—Marva N. Collins

15 Never let the fear of striking out get in your way.
—Babe Ruth

16 The greatest mistake you can make in life is continually to be fearing you will make one.
—Elbert Hubbard

1 A stumble may prevent a fall.
—ENGLISH PROVERB

2 He who never made a mistake never made a discovery.
—SAMUEL SMILES

3 A mistake proves that someone stopped talking long enough to do something.
—PHOENIX FLAME

4 Mistakes are the usual bridge between inexperience and wisdom.
—PHYLLIS THEROUX
Night Lights

5 Better to ask twice than to lose your way once.
—DANISH PROVERB

6 We're all proud of making little mistakes. It gives us the feeling we don't make any big ones.
—ANDREW A. ROONEY
Not That You Asked . . .

7 To err is human; to admit it, superhuman.
—DOUG LARSON

8 Admit your errors before someone else exaggerates them.
—ANDREW V. MASON, MD

9 There is no saint without a past— no sinner without a future.
—ANCIENT PERSIAN MASS

10 Once we realize that imperfect understanding is the human condition, there is no shame in being wrong, only in failing to correct our mistakes.
—GEORGE SOROS
Soros on Soros

11 One of the most dangerous forms of human error is forgetting what one is trying to achieve.
—PAUL NITZE

12 It is very easy to forgive others their mistakes; it takes more grit and gumption to forgive them for having witnessed your own.
—JESSAMYN WEST

13 The worst part is not in making a mistake but in trying to justify it, instead of using it as a heaven-sent warning of our mindlessness or our ignorance.
—SANTIAGO RAMÓN Y CAJAL
Charlas de Cafe

14 Always acknowledge a fault frankly. This will throw those in authority off their guard and give you opportunity to commit more.
—MARK TWAIN

15 To obtain maximum attention, it's hard to beat a good, big mistake.
—DAVID D. HEWITT

16 Justifying a fault doubles it.
—FRENCH PROVERB

1 Your worst humiliation is only someone else's momentary entertainment.

—KAREN CROCKETT

2 He who is afraid to ask is ashamed of learning.

—DANISH PROVERB

3 The only nice thing about being imperfect is the joy it brings to others.

—DOUG LARSON

4 Nine times out of ten, the first thing a man's companion knows of his shortcomings is from his apology.

—OLIVER WENDELL HOLMES SR.

5 If all else fails, immortality can always be assured by spectacular error.

—JOHN KENNETH GALBRAITH
Money: Whence It Came, Where It Went

I'D RATHER BE A FAILURE . . .

6 I'd rather be a failure at something I enjoy than be a success at something I hate.

—GEORGE BURNS

7 You never conquer a mountain. You stand on the summit a few moments; then the wind blows your footprints away.

—ARLENE BLUM

8 Victory is in the quality of competition, not the final score.

—MIKE MARSHALL

9 Laurels don't make much of a cushion.

—DOROTHY RABINOWITZ

10 Success covers a multitude of blunders.

—BERNARD SHAW

11 Failure is the condiment that gives success its flavor.

—TRUMAN CAPOTE

12 Success and failure. We think of them as opposites, but they're really not. They're companions— the hero and the sidekick.

—LAURENCE SHAMES

13 Don't confuse fame with success. Madonna is one; Helen Keller is the other.

—ERMA BOMBECK

14 The hero reveals the possibilities of human nature; the celebrity reveals the possibilities of the media.

—DANIEL J. BOORSTIN
The Image

15 Oh, the difference between nearly right and exactly right.

—HORACE J. BROWN

1 Success is never final, but failure can be.

—Bill Parcells
Finding a Way to Win

2 I couldn't wait for success . . . so I went ahead without it.

—Jonathan Winters

3 There is no comparison between that which is lost by not succeeding and that which is lost by not trying.

—Francis Bacon

4 You may be disappointed if you fail, but you are doomed if you don't try.

—Beverly Sills

5 Use what talents you possess: the woods would be very silent if no birds sang there except those that sang best.

—Henry Van Dyke

6 Ability is what you're capable of doing. Motivation determines what you do. Attitude determines how well you do it.

—Lou Holtz

7 True success is overcoming the fear of being unsuccessful.

—Paul Sweeney

8 If at first you do succeed—try to hide your astonishment.

—Los Angeles Times Syndicate

9 If you're not failing now and again, it's a sign you're playing it safe.

—Woody Allen

10 You're never as good as everyone tells you when you win, and you're never as bad as they say when you lose.

—Lou Holtz with John Heisler
The Fighting Spirit

11 It takes as much courage to have tried and failed as it does to have tried and succeeded.

—Anne Morrow Lindbergh

12 It isn't failing that spells one's downfall; it's running away, giving up.

—Michel Greco

13 If at first you don't succeed, try, try again. Then give up. There's no use in being a damn fool about it.

—W. C. Fields

14 Being defeated is often a temporary condition. Giving up is what makes it permanent.

—Marilyn vos Savant

15 On this earth, in the final analysis, each of us gets exactly what he deserves. But only the successful recognize this.

—Georges Simenon

1 If at first you don't succeed, you are running about average.

—M. H. ALDERSON

2 Success is not forever, and failure's not fatal.

—DON SHULA WITH KEN BLANCHARD
Everyone's a Coach

3 Failure is an event, never a person.

—WILLIAM D. BROWN
Welcome Stress!

4 Do not let what you cannot do interfere with what you can do.

—JOHN WOODEN
They Call Me Coach

5 Defeat may serve as well as victory to shake the soul and let the glory out.

—EDWIN MARKHAM

THE REWARD FOR WORK WELL DONE . . .

6 The reward for work well done is the opportunity to do more.

—JONAS SALK, MD

7 The reward of a thing well done is to have done it.

—RALPH WALDO EMERSON

8 Work is something you can count on, a trusted, lifelong friend who never deserts you.

—MARGARET BOURKE-WHITE

9 The biggest mistake you can make is to believe that you are working for someone else.

—*Bits & Pieces*

10 The work praises the man.

—IRISH PROVERB

11 One of the greatest sources of energy is pride in what you are doing.

—*SPOKES*

12 Do the best you can in every task, no matter how unimportant it may seem at the time. No one learns more about a problem than the person at the bottom.

—SANDRA DAY O'CONNOR

13 Manual labor to my father was not only good and decent for its own sake but, as he was given to saying, it straightened out one's thoughts.

—MARY ELLEN CHASE
A Goodly Fellowship

14 There's no labor a man can do that's undignified—if he does it right.

—BILL COSBY

15 Happiness, I have discovered, is nearly always a rebound from hard work.

—DAVID GRAYSON
Adventures in Contentment

1 There are no menial jobs, only menial attitudes.
—WILLIAM J. BENNETT
The Book of Virtues

2 Just as there are no little people or unimportant lives, there is no insignificant work.
—ELENA BONNER
Alone Together

3 There is a kind of victory in good work, no matter how humble.
—JACK KEMP

4 Thinking is the hardest work there is, which is probably the reason so few engage in it.
—HENRY FORD

5 Accomplishments have no color.
—LEONTYNE PRICE

6 The best preparation for work is not thinking about work, talking about work, or studying for work: it is work.
—WILLIAM WELD

7 Look at a day when you are supremely satisfied at the end. It's not a day when you lounge around doing nothing. It's when you've had everything to do, and you've done it.
—MARGARET THATCHER

8 The more I want to get something done, the less I call it work.
—RICHARD BACH
Illusions: The Adventures of a Reluctant Messiah

9 Nothing is work unless you'd rather be doing something else.
—GEORGE HALAS

10 My father always told me, "Find a job you love and you'll never have to work a day in your life."
—JIM FOX

11 When we do the best that we can, we never know what miracle is wrought in our life or in the life of another.
—HELEN KELLER

12 Ability will never catch up with the demand for it.
—MALCOLM S. FORBES

13 What you have inherited from your fathers, earn over again for yourselves, or it will not be yours.
—JOHANN WOLFGANG VON GOETHE

14 Not only is woman's work never done, the definition keeps changing.
—BILL COPELAND
in *Herald-Tribune* (Sarasota, Florida)

15 We work to become, not to acquire.
—ELBERT HUBBARD

1 Blessed is the person who is too busy to worry in the daytime and too sleepy to worry at night.

—LEO AIKMAN
in *Journal-Constitution* (Atlanta, Georgia)

2 Perfection is finally attained, not when there is no longer anything to add, but when there is no longer anything to take away.

—ANTOINE DE SAINT-EXUPÉRY

3 If you have a job without any aggravations, you don't have a job.

—MALCOLM S. FORBES

4 Work keeps us from three evils: boredom, vice and need.

—VOLTAIRE

5 It's strange how unimportant your job is when you're asking for a raise, but how important it can be when you want to take a day off.

—EARL A. MATHES
in *Tri-County Record* (Kiel, Wisconsin)

6 I don't know what liberation can do about it, but even when the man helps, woman's work is never done.

—BERYL PFIZER

7 The man who didn't want his wife to work has been succeeded by the man who asks about her chances of getting a raise.

—EARL WILSON

8 There is no such thing as a non-working mother.

—HESTER MUNDIS
Powermom

9 Work consists of whatever a body is obliged to do, and play consists of whatever a body is not obliged to do.

—MARK TWAIN
The Adventures of Tom Sawyer

10 Retirement, we understand, is great if you are busy, rich and healthy. But then, under those conditions, work is great too.

—BILL VAUGHAN

11 Retirement should be based on the tread, not the mileage.

—ALLEN LUDDEN

12 I don't want to achieve immortality through my work. I want to achieve immortality through not dying.

—WOODY ALLEN

13 It proves, on close examination, that work is less boring than amusing oneself.

—CHARLES BAUDELAIRE

EVERYWHERE IS WALKING DISTANCE . . .

14 Everywhere is walking distance if you have the time.

—STEVEN WRIGHT

1 The perfect journey is circular—
the joy of departure and the joy of
return.

—DINO BASILI
in *Il Tempe* (Rome, Itlay)

2 What is traveling? Changing your
place? By no means! Traveling is
changing your opinions and your
prejudices.

—ANATOLE FRANCE

3 The world is a book, and those
who do not travel read only one
page.

—ST. AUGUSTINE

4 There ain't no surer way to find
out whether you like people or
hate them than to travel with
them.

—MARK TWAIN

5 The rule for traveling abroad is to
take our common sense with us,
and leave our prejudices behind.

—WILLIAM HAZLITT

6 A good traveler is one who does
not know where he is going. A
perfect traveler does not know
where he came from.

—LIN YUTANG

7 Be careful going in search of
adventure—it's ridiculously easy to
find.

—WILLIAM LEAST HEAT MOON
Blue Highways: A Journey into America

8 Most travel is best of all in the
anticipation or the remembering;
the reality has more to do with
losing your luggage.

—REGINA NADELSON
in *European Travel & Life*

9 Thanks to the Interstate Highway
System, it is now possible to travel
across the country from coast to
coast without seeing anything.

—CHARLES KURALT
On the Road With Charles Kuralt

10 The average tourist wants to go to
places where there are no tourists.

—SAM EWING

11 Men travel faster now, but I do
not know if they go to better
things.

—WILLA CATHER
Death Comes for the Archbishop

12 Each year it seems to take less
time to fly across the ocean and
longer to drive to work.

—*The Globe and Mail* (Totonto, Ontario)

13 For travel to be delightful, one
must have a good place to leave
and return to.

—FREDERICK B. WILCOX

14 Traveling is like falling in love; the
world is made new.

—JAN MYRDAL

THE ART OF CONVERSATION

Words can sometimes, in moments of
grace, attain the quality of deeds.
—Elie Wiesel

IT'S A STRANGE WORLD OF LANGUAGE . . .

1 It's a strange world of language in which skating on thin ice can get you into hot water.
—FRANKLIN P. JONES
in *Quote*

2 If the English language made any sense, lackadaisical would have something to do with a shortage of flowers.
—DOUG LARSON

3 Words are vehicles that can transport us from the drab sands to the dazzling stars.
—M. ROBERT SYME

4 Words are like diamonds. Polish them too much, and all you get are pebbles.
—BRYCE COURTENAY

5 All words are pegs to hang ideas on.
—HENRY WARD BEECHER

6 Words can sometimes, in moments of grace, attain the quality of deeds.
—ELIE WIESEL

7 Words without ideas are like sails without wind.
—*Courier-Record* (Blackstone, Virginia)

8 A cliché is only something well said in the first place.
—BILL GRANGER
There Are No Spies

9 To "coin a phrase" is to place some value upon it.
—E. H. EVENSON

10 A different language is a different vision of life.
—FEDERICO FELLINI

11 Learn a new language and get a new soul.
—CZECH PROVERB

12 He who does not know foreign languages does not know anything about his own.
—JOHANN WOLFGANG VON GOETHE

13 It is often wonderful how putting down on paper a clear statement of a case helps one to see, not perhaps the way out, but the way in.
—A. C. BENSON

14 In certain trying circumstances, urgent circumstances, desperate circumstances, profanity furnishes a relief denied even to prayer.
—MARK TWAIN

15 Words, like eyeglasses, blur everything that they do not make more clear.
—JOSEPH JOUBERT

1 The two words "information" and "communication" are often used interchangeably, but they signify quite different things. Information is giving out; communication is getting through.

—SYDNEY J. HARRIS

2 Mincing your words makes it easier if you have to eat them later.

—FRANKLIN P. JONES

3 Man does not live by words alone, despite the fact that sometimes he has to eat them.

—ADLAI STEVENSON

4 When a man eats his words, that's recyling.

—FRANK A. CLARK

5 By inflection you can say much more than your words do.

—MALCOLM S. FORBES

6 Brevity may be the soul of wit, but not when someone's saying, "I love you."

—JUDITH VIORST

7 Words of comfort, skillfully administered, are the oldest therapy known to man.

—LOUIS NIZER

8 Be careful of your thoughts; they may become words at any moment.

—IARA GASSEN

9 Words, once they're printed, have a life of their own.

—CAROL BURNETT

10 Everything becomes a little different as soon as it is spoken out loud.

—HERMANN HESSE

11 If you wouldn't write it and sign it, don't say it.

—EARL WILSON

12 Among my most prized possessions are words that I have never spoken.

—ORSON REGA CARD

13 Words are as beautiful as wild horses, and sometimes as difficult to corral.

—TED BERKMAN
in *Christian Science Monitor*

14 Look out how you use proud words. When you let proud words go, it is not easy to call them back.

—CARL SANDBURG
Slabs of the Sunburnt West

15 North Americans communicate through buttons, T-shirts and bumper stickers the way some cultures use drums.

—TIM MCCARTHY

16 A spoken word is not a sparrow. Once it flies out, you can't catch it.

—RUSSIAN PROVERB

1 If you would be pungent, be brief; for it is with words as with sunbeams. The more they are condensed, the deeper they burn.
—ROBERT SOUTHEY

2 You can suffocate a thought by expressing it with too many words.
—FRANK A. CLARK

3 If it takes a lot of words to say what you have in mind, give it more thought.
—DENNIS ROTH

4 Say what you have to say, not what you ought.
—HENRY DAVID THOREAU

5 Why doesn't the fellow who says "I'm no speechmaker" let it go at that instead of giving a demonstration?
—KIN HUBBARD

6 The reason we make a long story short is so that we can tell another.
—SHARON SHOEMAKER

7 The most valuable of all talents is that of never using two words when one will do.
—THOMAS JEFFERSON

8 It's all right to hold a conversation, but you should let go of it now and then.
—RICHARD ARMOUR

To base thought only on speech is 9 to try nailing whispers to the wall. Writing freezes thought and offers it up for inspection.
—JACK ROSENTHAL
in *New York Times Magazine*

When the mouth stumbles, it is 10 worse than the foot.
—WEST AFRICAN PROVERB

One way to prevent conversation 11 from being boring is to say the wrong thing.
—FRANK SHEED

The first requirement of good con- 12 versation is that nobody should know what is coming next.
—HAVILAH BABCOCK

Conversation means being able 13 to disagree and still continue the discussion.
—DWIGHT MACDONALD

Candor is a compliment; it implies 14 equality. It's how true friends talk.
—PEGGY NOONAN
What I Saw at the Revolution

The genius of communication is 15 the ability to be both totally honest and totally kind at the same time.
—JOHN POWELL

Fine words butter no parsnips. 16
—ENGLISH PROVERB

1 To speak of "mere words" is much like speaking of "mere dynamite."
—C. J. Ducasse
in *The Key Reporter*

2 Words must surely be counted among the most powerful drugs man ever invented.
—Leo Rosten

3 Sticks and stones may break our bones, but words will break our hearts.
—Robert Fulghum
All I Really Need to Know I Learned in Kindergarten

4 The bitterest tears shed over graves are for words left unsaid and deeds left undone.
—Harriet Beecher Stowe

5 Do not the most moving moments of our lives find us all without words?
—Marcel Marceau

6 In prayer it is better to have a heart without words than words without a heart.
—John Bunyan

7 Sometimes good intentions and feelings are of greater moment than the awkwardness of their expression.
—Jonathan Yardley

8 Too much agreement kills a chat.
—Eldridge Cleaver
Soul on Ice

9 To touch a child's face, a dog's smooth coat, a petaled flower, the rough surface of a rock is to set up new orders of brain motion. To touch is to communicate.
—James W. Angell
Yes Is a World

10 What a wonderful thing is the mail, capable of conveying across continents a warm human handclasp.
—Quoted by Ranjan Bakshi

11 A letter is a soliloquy, but a letter with a postscript is a conversation.
—Lin Yutang

12 There is nothing like sealing a letter to inspire a fresh thought.
—Al Bernstein

13 It is a damned poor mind indeed that can't think of at least two ways of spelling any word.
—Andrew Jackson

14 Parents can plant magic in a child's mind through certain words spoken with some thrilling quality of voice, some uplift of the heart and spirit.
—Robert MacNeil
Wordstruck

1 A pun is a pistol let off at the ear; not a feather to tickle the intellect.

—CHARLES LAMB

SKILLFUL LISTENING IS THE BEST REMEDY . . .

2 Skillful listening is the best remedy for loneliness, loquaciousness and laryngitis.

—WILLIAM ARTHUR WARD
in *Tribune* (San Diego, California)

3 The greatest gift you can give another is the purity of your attention.

—RICHARD MOSS, MD

4 Listening, not imitation, may be the sincerest form of flattery.

—JOYCE BROTHERS

5 There is no greater loan than a sympathetic ear.

—FRANK TYGER
in *National Enquirer*

6 In order that all men may be taught to speak truth, it is necessary that all likewise should learn to hear it.

—SAMUEL JOHNSON

7 The less you talk, the more you're listened to.

—ABIGAIL VAN BUREN

8 Talk to a man about himself and he will listen for hours.

—BENJAMIN DISRAELI

9 Give every man thy ear but few thy voice.

—WILLIAM SHAKESPEARE

10 The most important thing in communication is to hear what isn't being said.

—PETER F. DRUCKER

11 Good communication is as stimulating as black coffee, and just as hard to sleep after.

—ANNE MORROW LINDBERGH
Gift From the Sea

12 There is always hope when people are forced to listen to both sides.

—JOHN STUART MILL

13 A good listener is not only popular everywhere, but after a while he knows something.

—WILSON MIZNER

14 Listen, or thy tongue will keep thee deaf.

—NATIVE AMERICAN PROVERB

15 No one really listens to anyone else. Try it for a while, and you'll see why.

—MIGNON MCLAUGHLIN

1 Listening to both sides of a story will convince you that there is more to a story than both sides.
—Frank Tyger

2 Sainthood emerges when you can listen to someone's tale of woe and not respond with a description of your own.
—Andrew V. Mason, MD

3 Most people would rather defend to the death your right to say it than listen to it.
—Robert Brault

4 To entertain some people all you have to do is listen.
—Bernard Edinger

5 Two great talkers will not travel far together.
—Spanish proverb

SILENCES MAKE THE REAL CONVERSATIONS . . .

6 Silences make the real conversations between friends. Not the saying but the never needing to say is what counts.
—Margaret Lee Runbeck
Answer Without Ceasing

7 Hospitality consists in a little fire, a little food and an immense quiet.
—Ralph Waldo Emerson

In quiet places, reason abounds. 8
—Adlai E. Stevenson

Well-timed silence is the most commanding expression. 9
—Mark Helprin
in The Wall Street Journal

There are times when silence has 10 the loudest voice.
—Leroy Brownlow
Today Is Mine

The time to stop talking is when 11 the other person nods his head affirmatively but says nothing.
—Henry S. Haskins
Meditations in Wall Street

The right word may be effective, 12 but no word was ever as effective as a rightly timed pause.
—Mark Twain

He approaches nearest to the gods 13 who knows how to be silent, even though he is in the right.
—Cato

Silence is the unbearable repartee. 14
—G. K. Chesterton

Silence is one of the hardest 15 arguments to refute.
—Josh Billings

Silence, along with modesty, is a 16 great aid to conversation.
—Montaigne

1 Silence is the safety zone of conversation.

—ARNOLD H. GLASOW

2 Silence is still a marvelous language that has few initiates.

—ROGER DUHAMEL
Lettres à une Provinciale

3 The most difficult thing in the world is to know how to do a thing and to watch someone else doing it wrong, without comment.

—THEODORE H. WHITE
in *The Atlantic*

4 Tact is the rare ability to keep silent while two friends are arguing, and you know both of them are wrong.

—HUGH ALLEN

5 Fools live to regret their words, wise men to regret their silence.

—WILL HENRY

6 Some people talk because they think sound is more manageable than silence.

—MARGARET HALSEY

7 Blessed are they who have nothing to say and who cannot be persuaded to say it.

—JAMES RUSSELL LOWELL

8 If you really want to keep a secret you don't need any help.

—O. A. CARPING

9 Isn't it strange that we talk least about the things we think about most!

—CHARLES A. LINDBERGH

10 A secret is what you tell someone else not to tell because you can't keep it to yourself.

—LEONARD LOUIS LEVINSON

11 The vanity of being known to be entrusted with a secret is generally one of the chief motives to disclose it.

—SAMUEL JOHNSON

12 None are so fond of secrets as those who do not mean to keep them.

—C. C. COLTON

13 The knowledge that a secret exists is half of the secret.

—JOSHUA MEYROWITZ
No Sense of Place

14 He who has a secret should not only hide it, but hide that he has it to hide.

—THOMAS CARLYLE

15 If you reveal your secrets to the wind, you should not blame the wind for revealing them to the trees.

—KAHLIL GIBRAN
Sand and Foam

1 No one keeps a secret better than he who ignores it.

—Louis-N. Fortin

2 Another person's secret is like another person's money: you are not as careful with it as you are with your own.

—E. W. Howe

3 Have you noticed that these days even a moment of silence has to be accompanied by background music?

—*Funny Funny World*

4 My personal hobbies are reading, listening to music and silence.

—Edith Sitwell

5 I like the silent church before the service begins better than any preaching.

—Ralph Waldo Emerson

BY EXPERT OPINION . . .

6 You can't always go by expert opinion. A turkey, if you ask a turkey, should be stuffed with grasshoppers, grit and worms.

—*Changing Times*

7 The man who never alters his opinion is like standing water, and breeds reptiles of the mind.

—William Blake

8 Opinions should be formed with great caution—and changed with greater.

—Josh Billings

9 A leading authority is anyone who has guessed right more than once.

—Frank A. Clark

10 It is only about things that do not interest one that one can give a really unbiased opinion, which is no doubt the reason why an unbiased opinion is always valueless.

—Oscar Wilde

11 We tolerate differences of opinion in people who are familiar to us. But differences of opinion in people we do not know sound like heresy or plots.

—Brooks Atkinson

12 The function of the expert is not to be more right than other people, but to be wrong for more sophisticated reasons.

—David Butler

13 An expert is someone called in at the last minute to share the blame.

—Sam Ewing
in *Mature Living*

14 Even when the experts all agree, they may well be mistaken.

—Bertrand Russell
The Skeptical Essays

1 Every man has a right to be wrong in his opinions. But no man has a right to be wrong in his facts.

—BERNARD BARUCH
The Public Years

2 It is easy enough to hold an opinion, but hard work to actually know what one is talking about.

—PAUL F. FORD
Companion to Narnia

3 Too often we enjoy the comfort of opinion without the discomfort of thought.

—JOHN F. KENNEDY

4 The fewer the facts, the stronger the opinion.

—ARNOLD H. GLASOW

5 The only thing worse than an expert is someone who thinks he's an expert.

—ALY A. COLON

6 A public-opinion poll is no substitute for thought.

—WARREN BUFFETT

7 Public opinion is like the castle ghost; no one has ever seen it, but everyone is scared of it.

—SIGMUND GRAFF

8 Every conviction was a whim at birth.

—HEYWOOD BROUN

9 Refusing to have an opinion is a way of having one, isn't it?

—LUIGI PIRANDELLO
Each in His Own Way

10 Saying what we think gives a wider range of conversation than saying what we know.

—CULLEN HIGHTOWER

11 To disagree, one doesn't have to be disagreeable.

—BARRY M. GOLDWATER WITH JACK CASSERLY
Goldwater

12 There's a difference between opinion and conviction. My opinion is something that is true for me personally; my conviction is something that is true for everybody—in my opinion.

—SYLVIA CORDWOOD

13 Every new opinion, at its starting, is precisely in a minority of one.

—THOMAS CARLYLE

ADMIRABLE ADVICE . . .

14 I sometimes give myself admirable advice, but I am incapable of taking it.

—MARY WORTLEY MONTAGU

15 To profit from good advice requires more wisdom than to give it.

—JOHN CHURTON COLLINS

1 You don't need to take a person's advice to make him feel good—just ask for it.

—LAURENCE J. PETER
Peter's Almanac

2 A knife of the keenest steel requires the whetstone, and the wisest man needs advice.

—ZOROASTER

3 Advice is an uncertain gift.

—WHITNEY JEFFERY

4 Expert advice is a great comfort, even when it's wrong.

—Quoted by ELLEN CURRIE
in *The New York Times*

5 When we ask for advice, we are usually looking for an accomplice.

—MARQUIS DE LA GRANGE

6 Advice is what we ask for when we already know the answer but wish we didn't.

—ERICA JONG

7 Most of us ask for advice when we know the answer but want a different one.

—IVERN BALL
in *National Enquirer*

8 Express an opinion, but send advice by freight.

—CHARLES CLARK MUNN

9 Good advice usually works best when preceded by a bad scare.

—AL BATT

10 Of the few innocent pleasures left to men past middle life, the jamming of common sense down the throats of fools is perhaps the keenest.

—T. H. HUXLEY

11 When we are well, we all have good advice for those who are ill.

—TERENCE

12 We are never so generous as when giving advice.

—FRANÇOIS DE LA ROCHEFOUCAULD

13 People who have what they want are fond of telling people who haven't what they want that they really don't want it.

—OGDEN NASH

14 We give advice by the bucket but take it by the grain.

—WILLIAM ALGER

15 The thing to do with good advice is to pass it on. It is never any good to oneself.

—OSCAR WILDE

16 Advice should always be consumed between two thick slices of doubt.

—WALT SCHMIDT
in *Parklabrea News*

1 The best advice yet given is that you don't have to take it.
—LIBBIE FUDIM

2 Don't be troubled if the temptation to give advice is irresistible; the ability to ignore it is universal.
—*Planned Security*

USE SOFT WORDS . . .

3 Use soft words and hard arguments.
—ENGLISH PROVERB

4 A good indignation makes an excellent speech.
—RALPH WALDO EMERSON

5 There is nothing in the world like a persuasive speech to fuddle the mental apparatus.
—MARK TWAIN

6 If you have an important point to make, don't try to be subtle or clever. Use a pile driver. Hit the point once. Then come back and hit it again. Then hit it a third time a tremendous whack.
—WINSTON CHURCHILL

7 Charm is a way of getting the answer yes without asking a clear question.
—ALBERT CAMUS
The Fall

Praise, like gold and diamonds, 8 owes its value only to its scarcity.
—SAMUEL JOHNSON

Sandwich every bit of criticism 9 between two layers of praise.
—MARY KAY ASH
Mary Kay on People Management

One thought driven home is better 10 than three left on base.
—JAMES LITER
in *National Enquirer*

Example is not the main thing in 11 influencing others. It is the only thing.
—ALBERT SCHWEITZER

THE GREAT CHARM IN ARGUMENT . . .

The great charm in argument is 12 really finding one's own opinions, not other people's.
—EVELYN WAUGH

It is better to debate a question 13 without settling it than to settle a question without debating it.
—JOSEPH JOUBERT

Nothing can keep an argument 14 going like two persons who aren't sure what they're arguing about.
—O. A. BATTISTA

1 A single fact will often spoil an interesting argument.
—*Selected Cryptograms III*

2 You have not converted a man because you have silenced him.
—John Morley

3 It is impossible to defeat an ignorant man in an argument.
—William G. McAdoo

4 In quarreling, the truth is always lost.
—Publilius Syrus

5 Never answer an angry word with an angry word. It's the second one that makes the quarrel.
—W. A. Nance

6 People generally quarrel because they cannot argue.
—G. K. Chesterton
More Quotable Chesterton

7 The difficult part in an argument is not to defend one's opinion but rather to know it.
—André Maurois

8 Quarrels would not last long if the fault were on one side only.
—François de La Rochefoucauld

9 Violence in the voice is often only the death rattle of reason in the throat.
—John F. Boyes

10 Whether on the road or in an argument, when you see red it's time to stop.
—Jan McKeithen

11 Anybody who thinks there aren't two sides to every argument is probably in one.
—*The Cockle Bur*

12 An apology is the superglue of life. It can repair just about anything.
—Lynn Johnston

13 The man who offers an insult writes it in sand, but for the man who receives it, it's chiseled in bronze.
—Giovanni Guareschi

14 An ounce of apology is worth a pound of loneliness.
—Joseph Joubert

15 An apology is a good way to have the last word.
—*Dell Crossword Puzzles*

PRAYER IS WHEN YOU TALK TO GOD . . .

16 Prayer is when you talk to God; meditation is when you listen to God.
—Quoted by Diana Robinson in *The People's Almanac*

1 Prayer is the key of the morning and the bolt of the evening.
—MOHANDAS K. GANDHI

2 The greatest prayer is patience.
—GAUTAMA BUDDHA

3 What we usually pray to God is not that His will be done, but that He approve ours.
—HELGA BERGOLD GROSS

4 The object of most prayers is to wangle an advance on good intentions.
—ROBERT BRAULT

5 Certain thoughts are prayers. There are moments when, whatever be the attitude of the body, the soul is on its knees.
—VICTOR HUGO

6 If you begin to live life looking for the God that is all around you, every moment becomes a prayer.
—FRANK BIANCO

7 Our prayers are answered not when we are given what we ask but when we are challenged to be what we can be.
—MORRIS ADLER

8 Any concern too small to be turned into a prayer is too small to be made into a burden.
—CORRIE TEN BOOM
Clippings from My Notebook

9 If we could all hear one another's prayers, God might be relieved of some of his burden.
—ASHLEIGH BRILLIANT

10 Serving God is doing good to man. But praying is thought an easier service and is therefore more generally chosen.
—BENJAMIN FRANKLIN

11 God is like a mirror. The mirror never changes but everybody who looks at it sees something different.
—Quoted by RABBI HAROLD KUSHNER
in *Ultimate Issues*

12 Prayer is less about changing the world than it is about changing ourselves.
—DAVID J. WOLPE
Teaching Your Children About God

13 Get down on your knees and thank God you are on your feet.
—IRISH SAYING

14 Never trust someone who has to change his tone to ask something of the Lord.
—ROBERTA A. EVERETT

15 Call on God, but row away from the rocks.
—ROBERT M. YOUNG

16 Trust in God—but tie your camel tight.
—PERSIAN PROVERB

CIVILATION'S GIFT

Civilization is a movement and not a condition, a voyage and not a harbor.

—Arnold Toynbee

GREAT IDEAS NEED LANDING GEAR . . .

1 Great ideas need landing gear as well as wings.

—C. D. JACKSON

2 The history of mankind is the history of ideas.

—LUDWIG VON MISES
Socialism: An Economic and Sociological Analysis

3 A man is but a product of his thoughts; what he thinks, that he becomes.

—MOHANDAS K. GANDHI

4 An invasion of armies can be resisted, but not an idea whose time has come.

—VICTOR HUGO

5 It is useless to send armies against ideas.

—GEORG BRANDES

6 Good ideas are not adopted automatically. They must be driven into practice with courageous impatience.

—ADM. HYMAN G. RICKOVER

7 A cup is useful only when it is empty; and a mind that is filled with beliefs, with dogmas, with assertions, with quotations is really an uncreative mind.

—J. KRISHNAMURTI

The man with a new idea is a crank until the idea succeeds. 8

—MARK TWAIN

The greatest discovery of my generation is that a human being can alter his life by altering his attitude. 9

—WILLIAM JAMES

Thought is action in rehearsal. 10

—SIGMUND FREUD

Change your thoughts and you change your world. 11

—REV. NORMAN VINCENT PEALE

He who cannot change the very fabric of his thought will never be able to change reality. 12

—ANWAR EL-SADAT

The mind is its own place, and in itself can make a heaven of hell, a hell of heaven. 13

—JOHN MILTON

If most of us are ashamed of shabby clothes and shoddy furniture, let us be more ashamed of shabby ideas and shoddy philosophies. 14

—ALBERT EINSTEIN

Civilization is a movement and not a condition, a voyage and not a harbor. 15

—ARNOLD TOYNBEE

1 Good thoughts bear good fruit,
bad thoughts bear bad fruit—and
man is his own gardener.

—JAMES ALLEN

2 Bring ideas in and entertain them
royally, for one of them may be
the king.

—MARK VAN DOREN

3 The test of a first-rate intelligence
is the ability to hold two opposed
ideas in the mind at the same
time, and still retain the ability
to function.

—F. SCOTT FITZGERALD

4 I like to have a man's knowledge
comprehend more than one class
of topics, one row of shelves. I
like a man who likes to see a fine
barn as well as a good tragedy.

—RALPH WALDO EMERSON

5 Learning is not attained by
chance. It must be sought for
with ardor and attended to with
diligence.

—ABIGAIL ADAMS

6 What we learn with pleasure we
never forget.

—ALFRED MERCIER

7 Most people are willing to pay
more to be amused than to be
educated.

—ROBERT C. SAVAGE
Life Lessons

8 Education is not training but
rather the process that equips you
to entertain yourself, a friend and
an idea.

—WALLACE STERLING

9 Education is not the filling of a
pail, but the lighting of a fire.

—WILLIAM BUTLER YEATS

10 There are two ways of spreading
light: to be the candle or the
mirror that reflects it.

—EDITH WHARTON

11 An education is like a crumbling
building that needs constant
upkeep with repairs and additions.

—LOUIS DUDEK

12 A master can tell you what he
expects of you. A teacher, though,
awakens your own expectations.

—PATRICIA NEAL WITH RICHARD DENEUT
As I Am: An Autobiography

13 A great teacher never strives to
explain his vision—he simply
invites you to stand beside him
and see for yourself.

—REV. R. INMAN

14 If you would thoroughly know
anything, teach it to others.

—TRYON EDWARDS

15 To teach is to learn twice.

—JOSEPH JOUBERT

1 Good education is the essential foundation of a strong democracy.
—BARBARA BUSH
in a preface to *America's Country Schools* by Andrew Gulliford

2 Education is more than a luxury; it is a responsibility that society owes to itself.
—ROBIN COOK
Coma

3 Education is learning what you didn't even know you didn't know.
—DANIEL J. BOORSTIN
Democracy and Its Discontents

4 Without education, we are in a horrible and deadly danger of taking educated people seriously.
—G. K. CHESTERTON

5 It is not the business of science to inherit the earth, but to inherit the moral imagination; because without that, man and beliefs and science will perish together.
—JACOB BRONOWSKI

6 Science has made us gods even before we are worthy of being men.
—JEAN ROSTAND

7 An age is called Dark, not because the light fails to shine, but because people refuse to see it.
—JAMES A. MICHENER
Space

8 In every work of genius, we recognize our own rejected thoughts; they come back to us with a certain alienated majesty.
—RALPH WALDO EMERSON

9 If you are seeking creative ideas, go out walking. Angels whisper to a man when he goes for a walk.
—RAYMOND INMAN

10 An idea can turn to dust or magic, depending on the talent that rubs against it.
—WILLIAM BERNBACH

11 Be curious always! For knowledge will not acquire you; you must acquire it.
—SUDIE BACK

12 Curiosity is the wick in the candle of learning.
—WILLIAM A. WARD

13 The little I know, I owe to my ignorance.
—SACHA GUITRY

14 Curiosity is a willing, a proud, an eager confession of ignorance.
—S. LEONARD RUBINSTEIN
Writing: A Habit of Mind

15 A sense of curiosity is nature's original school of education.
—SMILEY BLANTON, MD
Love or Perish

1 The human mind is as driven to understand as the body is driven to survive.

—HUGH GILMORE
in *The Philadelphia Inquirer Magazine*

2 If a man had as many ideas during the day as he does when he has insomnia, he'd make a fortune.

—GRIFF NIBLACK
in *News* (Indianapolis, Indiana)

3 Ideas are like rabbits. You get a couple and learn how to handle them, and pretty soon you have a dozen.

—JOHN STEINBECK

4 All my best thoughts were stolen by the ancients.

—RALPH WALDO EMERSON

5 A new idea is delicate. It can be killed by a sneer or a yawn; it can be stabbed to death by a quip, and worried to death by a frown on the right man's brow.

—CHARLIE BROWER

6 Man's mind stretched to a new idea never goes back to its original dimensions.

—OLIVER WENDELL HOLMES

7 One should never spoil a good theory by explaining it.

—PETER MCARTHUR

8 Once a new idea springs into existence, it cannot be unthought. There is a sense of immortality in a new idea.

—EDWARD DE BONO
New Think: The Use of Lateral Thinking in the Generation of New Ideas

9 An open mind collects more riches than an open purse.

—WILL HENRY

10 A cold in the head causes less suffering than an idea.

—JULES RENARD

READING FURNISHES THE MIND . . .

11 Reading furnishes the mind only with materials of knowledge; it is thinking that makes what we read ours.

—JOHN LOCKE

12 Reading is to the mind what exercise is to the body.

—JOSEPH ADDISON

13 Books may well be the only true magic.

—ALICE HOFFMAN

14 Books are not made for furniture, but there is nothing else that so beautifully furnishes a house.

—HENRY WARD BEECHER

1 Reading makes immigrants of us all—it takes us away from home, but more important, it finds homes for us everywhere.

—HAZEL ROCHMAN
Against Borders

2 There are perhaps no days of our childhood we lived so fully as those we believe we left without having lived them: those we spent with a favorite book.

—MARCEL PROUST

3 From your parents you learn love and laughter and how to put one foot before the other. But when books are opened you discover that you have wings.

—HELEN HAYES WITH SANDFORD DODY
On Reflection

4 Books are the carriers of civilization. Without books, history is silent, literature dumb, science crippled, thought and speculation at a standstill.

—BARBARA W. TUCHMAN

5 Books had instant replay long before televised sports.

—BERN WILLIAMS

6 If you would understand your own age, read the works of fiction produced in it. People in disguise speak freely.

—ARTHUR HELPS
Thoughts in the Cloister and the Crowd

7 Books are more than books. They are the life, the very heart and core of ages past, the reason why men lived and worked and died, the essence and quintessence of their lives.

—AMY LOWELL

8 There are no faster or firmer friendships than those between people who love the same books.

—IRVING STONE

9 Every man who knows how to read has it in his power to magnify, to multiply the ways in which he exists, to make his life full, significant and interesting.

—ALDOUS HUXLEY

10 Fiction reveals truths that reality obscures.

—JESSAMYN WEST

11 Reading without reflecting is like eating without digesting.

—EDMUND BURKE

12 No one ever really paid the price of a book—only the price of printing it.

—LOUIS I. KAHN

13 A truly good book is something as wildly natural and primitive, mysterious and marvelous, ambrosial and fertile as a fungus or a lichen.

—HENRY DAVID THOREAU

1 I would rather be a poor man in a garret with plenty of books than a king who did not love reading.
—Thomas Babington Macaulay

2 My test of a good novel is dreading to begin the last chapter.
—Thomas Helm

3 A book is a success when people who haven't read it pretend they have.
—Los Angeles Times Syndicate

4 If you would know what nobody knows, read what everybody reads, just one year afterward.
—Ralph Waldo Emerson

5 I divide all readers into two classes: those who read to remember and those who read to forget.
—William Lyon Phelps

6 The wise man reads both books and life itself.
—Lin Yutang

7 The library is the temple of learning, and learning has liberated more people than all the wars in history.
—Carl Rowan

8 The real purpose of books is to trap the mind into doing its own thinking.
—Christopher Morley

9 Without libraries what have we? We have no past and no future.
—Ray Bradbury

10 Perhaps no place in any community is so totally democratic as the town library. The only entrance requirement is interest.
—Lady Bird Johnson

11 A book should serve as the ax for the frozen sea within us.
—Franz Kafka

12 A well-composed book is a magic carpet on which we are wafted to a world that we cannot enter in any other way.
—Caroline Gordon
How to Read a Novel

13 You know you've read a good book when you turn the last page and feel a little as if you have lost a friend.
—Paul Sweeney

14 Books support us in our solitude and keep us from being a burden to ourselves.
—Jeremy Collier

15 There is a wonder in reading braille that the sighted will never know: to touch words and have them touch you back.
—Jim Fiebig

1 A book, tight shut, is but a block of paper.
—CHINESE PROVERB

2 A great book should leave you with many experiences and slightly exhausted at the end. You live several lives while reading it.
—WILLIAM STYRON

3 A truly great book should be read in youth, again in maturity and once more in old age, as a fine building should be seen by morning light, at noon and by moonlight.
—ROBERTSON DAVIES
The Enthusiasms of Robertson Davies

4 "Tell me what you read and I'll tell you who you are" is true enough, but I'd know you better if you told me what you reread.
—FRANÇOIS MAURIAC

5 When something can be read without effort, great effort has gone into its writing.
—ENRIQUE JARDIEL PONCELA

6 Wherever they burn books they will also, in the end, burn human beings.
—HEINRICH HEINE

7 You don't have to burn books to destroy a culture. Just get people to stop reading them.
—RAY BRADBURY

8 An author retains the singular distinction of being the only person who can remain a bore long after he is dead.
—SYDNEY J. HARRIS

9 For a man to become a poet he must be in love, or miserable.
—GEORGE GORDON, LORD BYRON

10 You don't have to suffer to be a poet. Adolescence is enough suffering for anyone.
—JOHN CIARDI

11 In the end, the poem is not a thing we see; it is, rather, a light by which we may see—and what we see is life.
—ROBERT PENN WARREN

12 Poetry is language at its most distilled and most powerful.
—RITA DOVE

13 A poem begins in delight and ends in wisdom.
—ROBERT FROST

14 Poetry is an echo, asking a shadow to dance.
—CARL SANDBURG

15 The difference between reality and fiction? Fiction has to make sense.
—TOM CLANCY

1 Choose an author as you choose a
friend.

—WENTWORTH DILLON

2 Fable is more historical than fact,
because fact tells us about one
man and fable tells us about a
million men.

—G. K. CHESTERTON

3 Let us read and let us dance—two
amusements that will never do
any harm to the world.

—VOLTAIRE

4 I cannot conceive how a novelist
could fail to pity or love the
smallest creation of his imagination; incomplete as these characters may be, they are the writer's
bond with the real world, its
suffering and heartbreak.

—GABRIELLE ROY
*The Fragile Lights Of Earth: Articles And
Memories 1942–1970*

5 When you take stuff from one
writer, it's plagiarism; but when
you take it from many writers it's
research.

—WILSON MIZNER

6 October is crisp days and cool
nights, a time to curl up around
the dancing flames and sink into
a good book.

—JOHN SINOR
in *Union-Tribune* (San Diego, California)

There's nothing to writing. All you 7
do is sit down at a typewriter and
open a vein.

—RED SMITH

When I want to read a novel, I 8
write one.

—BENJAMIN DISRAELI

ART IS A STAPLE, LIKE BREAD . . .

Art is a staple, like bread or wine 9
or a warm coat in winter. Man's
spirit grows hungry for art in the
same way his stomach growls for
food.

—IRVING STONE
Depths of Glory

Art is the signature of civilization. 10

—BEVERLY SILLS

Art extends each man's short time 11
on earth by carrying from man
to man the whole complexity of
other men's lifelong experience,
with all its burdens, colors and
flavor.

—ALEKSANDR SOLZHENITSYN
One Word of Truth . . .

Every fragment of song holds 12
a mirror to a past moment for
someone.

—FANNY CRADOCK
War Comes to Castle Rising

1 A room hung with pictures is a
room hung with thoughts.
—SIR JOSHUA REYNOLDS

2 Anyone who says you can't see a
thought simply doesn't know art.
—WYNETKA ANN REYNOLDS

3 No great artist ever sees things as
they really are. If he did, he
would cease to be an artist.
—OSCAR WILDE

4 Art is the demonstration that the
ordinary is extraordinary.
—AMÉDÉE OZENFANT
Foundations of Modern Art

5 Art doesn't reproduce the visible
but rather makes it visible.
—PAUL KLEE

6 It has been said that art is a tryst;
for the joy of it maker and
beholder meet.
—KOJIRO TOMITA

7 Art is the only way to run away
without leaving home.
—TWYLA THARP

8 Half of art is knowing when to
stop.
—ARTHUR WILLIAM RADFORD

9 The other arts persuade us, but
music takes us by surprise.
—EDUARD HANSLICK

10 Without music, life is a journey
through a desert.
—PAT CONROY
Beach Music

11 Country music is three chords and
the truth.
—HARLAN HOWARD

12 Music is the way our memories
sing to us across time.
—LANCE MORROW
in *Time*

13 After silence, that which comes
nearest to expressing the
inexpressible is music.
—ALDOUS HUXLEY
Music at Night and Other Essays

14 Music washes away from the soul
the dust of everyday life.
—BERTHOLD AUERBACH

15 Music is the shorthand of emotion.
—LEO TOLSTOY

16 Where words fail, music speaks.
—HANS CHRISTIAN ANDERSEN

17 Music is a higher revelation than
philosophy.
—LUDWIG VAN BEETHOVEN

18 People who make music together
cannot be enemies, at least not
while the music lasts.
—PAUL HINDEMITH

1 He who sings frightens away his ills.
—MIGUEL DE CERVANTES SAAVEDRA

2 God respects me when I work,
but he loves me when I sing.
—RABINDRANATH TAGORE

3 If I may venture my own definition of a folk song, I should call it
"an individual flowering on a
common stem."
—RALPH VAUGHN WILLIAMS

4 Learning music by reading about
it is like making love by mail.
—LUCIANO PAVAROTTI

5 No one should be allowed to play
the violin until he has mastered it.
—JIM FIEBIG

6 Those move easiest who have
learned to dance.
—ALEXANDER POPE

7 The truest expression of a people
is in its dances and its music.
Bodies never lie.
—AGNES DE MILLE

8 Inside every man there is a poet
who died young.
—STEPHAN KANFER

9 There is no abstract art. You must
always start with something.
Afterward you can remove all
traces of reality.
—PABLO PICASSO

10 Every artist was first an amateur.
—RALPH WALDO EMERSON

11 The greatest artist was once a
beginner.
—Farmer's Digest

12 All art, like all love, is rooted in
heartache.
—ALFRED STIEGLITZ

13 What art offers is space—a certain
breathing room for the spirit.
—JOHN UPDIKE

14 More important than a work of art
itself is what it will sow. Art can
die, a painting can disappear.
What counts is the seed.
—JOAN MIRÓ

15 Art is the triumph over chaos.
—JOHN CHEEVER

16 What is art but a way of seeing?
—THOMAS BERGER
Being Invisible

17 A great artist is never poor.
—ISAK DINESEN
Anecdotes of Destiny

18 Talent is a flame. Genius is a fire.
—BERN WILLIAMS

19 No one can arrive from being
talented alone. God gives talent;
work transforms talent into genius.
—ANNA PAVLOVA

1 Discipline is the refining fire by which talent becomes ability.
—ROY L. SMITH

2 Perfectionism is the enemy of creation, as extreme self-solicitude is the enemy of well-being.
—JOHN UPDIKE
Odd Jobs

3 When love and skill work together, expect a masterpiece.
—JOHN RUSKIN

4 I created nothing; I invented nothing; I imagined nothing; I perverted nothing; I simply discovered drama in real life.
—BERNARD SHAW

5 There's no need to believe what an artist says. Believe what he does; that's what counts.
—DAVID HOCKNEY

6 Every child is an artist. The problem is how to remain an artist once he grows up.
—PABLO PICASSO

7 Really we create nothing. We merely plagiarize nature.
—JEAN BAITAILLON

8 A great city is one that handles its garbage and art equally well.
—BOB TALBERT

9 A good snapshot stops a moment from running away.
—EUDORA WELTY

10 The cinema has no boundary; it is a ribbon of dream.
—ORSON WELLES

11 Of course, there must be subtleties. Just make sure you make them obvious.
—BILLY WILDER

12 It pays to be obvious, especially if you have a reputation for subtlety.
—ISAAC ASIMOV
Foundation

13 Simplicity, carried to an extreme, becomes elegance.
—JON FRANKLIN
Writing for Story

14 It is only by introducing the young to great literature, drama and music, and to the excitement of great science that we open to them the possibilities that lie within the human spirit — enable them to see visions and dream dreams.
—ERIC ANDERSON

15 Man creates culture and through culture creates himself.
—POPE JOHN PAUL II
in *Osservatore Romano*

THE NATURE
OF LIFE

*The way I see it, if you want the rainbow,
you gotta put up with the rain.*

—Dolly Parton

IN THE LONG ETERNITY OF TIME . . .

1 It is easier to accept the message of the stars than the message of the salt desert. The stars speak of man's insignificance in the long eternity of time; the deserts speak of his insignificance right now.

—EDWIN WAY TEALE

2 Eternity is a terrible thought. I mean, where's it going to end?

—TOM STOPPARD

3 Forever is a long time, but not as long as it was yesterday.

—DENNIS H'ORGNIES

4 Time is but the stream I go a-fishing in.

—HENRY DAVID THOREAU

5 Time neither subtracts nor divides, but adds at such a pace it seems like multiplication.

—BOB TALBERT

6 The future is the past returning through another gate.

—ARNOLD H. GLASOW

7 Snatching the eternal out of the desperately fleeting is the great magic trick of human existence.

—TENNESSEE WILLIAMS
in *The New York Times*

8 Time is a versatile performer. It flies, marches on, heals all wounds, runs out and will tell.

—FRANKLIN P. JONES

9 Time goes, you say? Ah, no! Alas, Time stays, we go.

—AUSTIN DOBSON

10 Time marks us while we are marking time.

—THEODORE ROETHKE
Straw for the Fire

11 Time wastes our bodies and our wits, but we waste time, so we are quits.

—*Verse and Worse*

12 In rivers, the water that you touch is the last of what has passed and the first of that which comes: so with present time.

—LEONARDO DA VINCI

13 You don't get to choose how you're going to die. Or when. You can only decide how you're going to live. Now.

—JOAN BAEZ

14 The feeling of being hurried is not usually the result of living a full life and having no time. It is, rather, born of a vague fear that we are wasting our life.

—ERIC HOFFER

1 Yesterday is a canceled check; tomorrow is a promissory note; today is ready cash—use it.

—KAY LYONS

2 How you spend your time is more important than how you spend your money. Money mistakes can be corrected, but time is gone forever.

—DAVID B. NORRIS

3 Those who make the worst use of their time are the first to complain of its shortness.

—JEAN DE LA BRUYÈRE

4 Half our life is spent trying to find something to do with the time we have rushed through life trying to save.

—WILL ROGERS

5 Today's greatest labor-saving device is tomorrow.

—TOM WILSON

6 Mañana is often the busiest day of the week.

—SPANISH PROVERB

7 One of these days is none of these days.

—HENRI TUBACH

8 By the streets of "by and by" one arrives at the house of "never."

—SPANISH PROVERB

9 Don't put off for tomorrow what you can do today, because if you enjoy it today you can do it again tomorrow.

—JAMES A. MICHENER

10 Nothing adds to a person's leisure time like doing things when they are supposed to be done.

—O. A. BATTISTA

11 For disappearing acts, it's hard to beat what happens to the eight hours supposedly left after eight of sleep and eight of work.

—DOUG LARSON

12 When we don't waste time, we always have enough.

—JEAN DRAPEAU

13 As if we could kill time without injuring eternity!

—HENRY DAVID THOREAU

14 A man who has to be punctually at a certain place at five o'clock has the whole afternoon ruined for him already.

—LIN YUTANG
The Importance of Living

15 The surest way to be late is to have plenty of time.

—LEO KENNEDY

16 Normal day, let me be aware of the treasure you are.

—MARY JEAN IRION

1 Butterflies count not months but moments, and yet have time enough.

—RABINDRANATH TAGORE

2 Time, for all its smuggling in of new problems, conspicuously cancels others.

—CLARA WINSTON
in *The Massachusetts Review*

3 Time has a wonderful way of weeding out the trivial.

—RICHARD BEN SAPIR
Quest

4 I still find each day too short for all the thoughts I want to think, all the walks I want to take, all the books I want to read and all the friends I want to see.

—JOHN BURROUGHS

5 Yesterday is experience. Tomorrow is hope. Today is getting from one to the other as best we can.

—JOHN M. HENRY

6 You must have been warned against letting the golden hours slip by; but some of them are golden only because we let them slip by.

—JAMES M. BARRIE

7 We are tomorrow's past.

—MARY WEBB
Precious Bane

8 The present is the point at which time touches eternity.

—C. S. LEWIS
Screwtape Letters

9 Life is uncharted territory. It reveals its story one moment at a time.

—LEO BUSCAGLIA
in *Executive Health Report*

10 I never think of the future. It comes soon enough.

—ALBERT EINSTEIN

11 There is no distance on this earth as far away as yesterday.

—ROBERT NATHAN
So Love Returns

12 The past is really almost as much a work of the imagination as the future.

—JESSAMYN WEST

13 He who believes that the past cannot be changed has not yet written his memoirs.

—TORVALD GAHLIN

14 There is a time to let things happen and a time to make things happen.

—HUGH PRATHER
Notes on Love and Courage

15 Every man regards his own life as the New Year's Eve of time.

—JEAN PAUL RICHTER

1 The best thing about the future is
that it comes only one day at a
time.
—DEAN ACHESON

2 I love best to have each thing in
its season, doing without it at all
other times.
—HENRY DAVID THOREAU

3 Life is not dated merely by years.
Events are sometimes the best
calendars.
—BENJAMIN DISRAELI

4 Time has no divisions to mark its
passage; there is never a thunder-
storm to announce the beginning
of a new year. It is only we
mortals who ring bells and fire
off pistols.
—THOMAS MANN

5 Life is not a "brief candle." It is
a splendid torch that I want to
make burn as brightly as possible
before handing it on to future
generations.
—BERNARD SHAW

ALL THE ART OF LIVING . . .

6 All the art of living lies in a fine
mingling of letting go and
holding on.
—HAVELOCK ELLIS

God asks no man whether he will 7
accept life. That is not the choice.
One must take it. The only choice
is how.
—HENRY WARD BEECHER

If we live good lives, the times are 8
also good. As we are, such are the
times.
—ST. AUGUSTINE

We are here to add what we can 9
to, not to get what we can from,
life.
—SIR WILLIAM OSLER

Presence is more than just being 10
there.
—MALCOLM S. FORBES
*The Further Sayings of Chairman
Malcolm*

There are three things that if a 11
man does not know, he cannot
live long in this world: what is too
much for him, what is too little for
him and what is just right for him.
—SWAHILI PROVERB

You only live once. But if you 12
work it right, once is enough.
—FRED ALLEN

Besides the noble art of getting 13
things done, there is the noble art
of leaving things undone. The
wisdom of life consists in the
elimination of non-essentials.
—LIN YUTANG

1 There is more to life than increasing its speed.

—Mohandas K. Gandhi

2 Everything should be made as simple as possible, but not simpler.

—Albert Einstein

3 I believe the art of living consists not so much in complicating simple things as in simplifying things that are not.

—François Hertel

4 Simplicity is making the journey of this life with just baggage enough.

—Charles Dudley Warner

5 Seize from every moment its unique novelty, and do not prepare your joys.

—André Gide
Nourritures Terrestres

6 Excess on occasion is exhilarating. It prevents moderation from acquiring the deadening effect of a habit.

—W. Somerset Maugham

7 If you can spend a perfectly useless afternoon in a perfectly useless manner, you have learned how to live.

—Lin Yutang

8 He does not seem to me to be a free man who does not sometimes do nothing.

—Cicero

9 How we spend our days is, of course, how we spend our lives.

—Annie Dillard
The Writing Life

10 A holiday gives one a chance to look backward and forward, to reset oneself by an inner compass.

—May Sarton
At Seventy (A Journal)

11 The time to relax is when you don't have time for it.

—Sydney J. Harris

12 A vacation is having nothing to do and all day to do it in.

—Robert Orben

13 The discovery of a new dish does more for human happiness than the discovery of a star.

—Anthelme Brillat-Savarin

14 A good cook is like a sorceress who dispenses happiness.

—Elsa Schiaparelli

15 There is no love sincerer than the love of food.

—Bernard Shaw

1 We never repent of having eaten too little.

—THOMAS JEFFERSON

2 One of the very nicest things about life is the way we must regularly stop whatever it is we are doing and devote our attention to eating.

—LUCIANO PAVAROTTI WITH WILLIAM WRIGHT
Pavarotti, My Own Story

3 There is a sufficiency in the world for man's need but not for man's greed.

—MOHANDAS K. GANDHI

4 Whatever will satisfy hunger is good food.

—CHINESE PROVERB

5 'Tis an ill cook that cannot lick his own fingers.

—WILLIAM SHAKESPEARE

6 One must ask children and birds how cherries and strawberries taste.

—JOHANN WOLFGANG VON GOETHE

7 Never eat more than you can lift.

—*Miss Piggy's Guide to Life*,
as told to Henry Beard

8 There is only one difference between a long life and a good dinner: that, in the dinner, the sweets come last.

—ROBERT LOUIS STEVENSON

9 We are all mortal until the first kiss and the second glass of wine.

—EDUARDO GALEANO
The Book of Embraces

10 Be glad of life because it gives you the chance to love and to work and to play and to look up at the stars.

—HENRY VAN DYKE

11 The art of living is more like wrestling than dancing.

—MARCUS AURELIUS

12 Part of the art of living is knowing how to compare yourself with the right people. Dissatisfaction is often the result of unsuitable comparison.

—DR. HEINRICH SOBOTKA
Madame

13 Is not life a hundred times too short for us to bore ourselves?

—FRIEDRICH NIETZSCHE

14 Enjoy the little things, for one day you may look back and realize they were the big things.

—ROBERT BRAULT
in *National Enquirer*

15 Yes, there is a nirvana; it is in leading your sheep to a green pasture, and in putting your child to sleep, and in writing the last line of your poem.

—KAHLIL GIBRAN

1 When things start going your way, it's usually because you stopped going the wrong way down a one-way street.

—Los Angeles Times Syndicate

2 One ought, every day at least, to hear a little song, read a good poem, see a fine picture and, if possible, speak a few reasonable words.

—Johann Wolfgang von Goethe

IDEALS ARE LIKE THE STARS . . .

3 Ideals are like the stars. We never reach them but, like the mariners on the sea, we chart our course by them.

—Carl Schurz

4 The ideals which have lighted my way, and time after time have given me new courage to face life cheerfully, have been kindness, beauty and truth.

—Albert Einstein
Ideas and Opinions

5 When you teach your son, you teach your son's son.

—The Talmud

6 The true idealist pursues what his heart says is right in a way that his head says will work.

—Richard M. Nixon

7 If things were really as we wanted them to be, people would still complain that they were no longer what they used to be.

—Pierre Dac

8 I am an idealist. I don't know where I'm going, but I'm on my way.

—Carl Sandburg

SOME THINGS HAVE TO BE BELIEVED . . .

9 Some things have to be believed to be seen.

—Ralph Hodgson
The Skylark and Other Poems

10 One person with a belief is a social power equal to 99 who have only interests.

—John Stuart Mill

11 To believe with certainty, we must begin with doubting.

—Stanislaus I

12 Faith is building on what you know is here, so you can reach what you know is there.

—Cullen Hightower

13 Strike from mankind the principle of faith and men would have no more history than a flock of sheep.

—Mark Beltaire

1 Science is not only compatible with spirituality; it is a profound source of spirituality.

—CARL SAGAN
The Demon-Haunted World: Science as a Candle in the Dark

2 If we were logical, the future would be bleak indeed. But we are more than logical. We are human beings, and we have faith, and we have hope, and we can work.

—JACQUES COUSTEAU

3 We couldn't conceive of a miracle if none had ever happened.

—LIBBIE FUDIM

4 In faith there is enough light for those who want to believe and enough shadows to blind those who don't.

—BLAISE PASCAL

5 All I have seen teaches me to trust the Creator for all I have not seen.

—RALPH WALDO EMERSON

6 Faith is knowing there is an ocean because you have seen a brook.

—WILLIAM ARTHUR WARD

7 Faith is like radar that sees through the fog—the reality of things at a distance that the human eye cannot see.

—CORRIE TEN BOOM
Tramp for the Lord

8 Faith is the bird that sings when the dawn is still dark.

—RABINDRANATH TAGORE

9 What I admire in Columbus is not his having discovered a world but his having gone to search for it on the faith of an opinion.

—A. ROBERT TURGOT

10 If the stars should appear just one night in a thousand years, how would men believe and adore!

—RALPH WALDO EMERSON

11 Many of us look at the Ten Commandments as an exam paper: eight only to be attempted.

—MALCOLM MUGGERIDGE
Reality Ireland

12 The finest fruit of serious learning should be the ability to speak the word God without reserve or embarrassment.

—NATHAN M. PUSEY

13 Our rabbi once said, "God always answers our prayers, it's just that sometimes the answer is no."

—BARBARA FEINSTEIN

14 If you are not as close to God as you used to be, who moved?

—*St. Mathias' Church Bulletin*

15 Sorrow looks back, worry looks around, faith looks up.

—Quoted in *Guideposts Magazine*

1 It is good enough to talk of God while we are sitting here after a nice breakfast and looking forward to a nicer luncheon, but how am I to talk of God to the millions who have to go without two meals a day? To them God can only appear as bread and butter.

—Mohandas K. Gandhi

2 Real religion is a way of life, not a white cloak to be wrapped around us on the Sabbath and then cast aside into the six-day closet of unconcern.

—William Arthur Ward
Think It Over

HOPE IS THE THING WITH FEATHERS . . .

3 Hope is the thing with feathers that perches in the soul.

—Emily Dickinson

4 Hope smiles on the threshold of the year to come, whispering that it will be happier.

—Alfred, Lord Tennyson

5 He who has health has hope, and he who has hope has everything.

—Arab proverb

6 The natural flights of the human mind are not from pleasure to pleasure but from hope to hope.

—Samuel Johnson

7 Hope is not the conviction that something will turn out well but the certainty that something makes sense, regardless of how it turns out.

—Vaclav Havel
Disturbing the Peace

8 There is one thing which gives radiance to everything. It is the idea of something around the corner.

—G. K. Chesterton

9 Waiting is still an occupation. It is not having anything to wait for that is terrible.

—Cesare Pavese
Il Mestiere di Vivere

10 We must learn to reawaken and keep ourselves awake, not by mechanical aids, but by an infinite expectation of the dawn.

—Henry David Thoreau

11 In every winter's heart there is a quivering spring, and behind the veil of each night there is a smiling dawn.

—Kahlil Gibran

12 Sometimes our fate resembles a fruit tree in winter. Who would think that those branches would turn green again and blossom, but we hope it, we know it.

—Johann Wolfgang von Goethe

1 A ship should not ride on a single anchor, nor life on a single hope.
—EPICTETUS

2 We must accept finite disappointment, but we must never lose infinite hope.
—REV. MARTIN LUTHER KING JR.

3 There are no hopeless situations; there are only people who have grown hopeless about them.
—CLARE BOOTHE LUCE

4 I have always been delighted at the prospect of a new day, a fresh try, one more start, with perhaps a bit of magic waiting somewhere behind the morning.
—J. B. PRIESTLEY

5 In the face of uncertainty, there is nothing wrong with hope.
—BERNIE SIEGEL
Love, Medicine and Miracles

6 When you say a situation or a person is hopeless, you are slamming the door in the face of God.
—REV. CHARLES L. ALLEN

7 There is no better or more blessed bondage than to be a prisoner of hope.
—ROY Z. KEMP

THE KIND OF BEAUTY I WANT . . .

The kind of beauty I want most is 8 the hard-to-get kind that comes from within—strength, courage, dignity.
—RUBY DEE

Some people, no matter how old 9 they get, never lose their beauty— they merely move it from their faces into their hearts.
—MARTIN BUXBAUM
in *National Enquirer*

Love beauty; it is the shadow of 10 God on the universe.
—GABRIELA MISTRAL
Desolacíon

Though we travel the world over 11 to find the beautiful, we must carry it with us or we find it not.
—RALPH WALDO EMERSON

Taking joy in living is a woman's 12 best cosmetic.
—ROSALIND RUSSELL

Tell a girl she's beautiful, and she 13 wouldn't believe you really mean it. Tell her she's more beautiful than another girl, and she would delightfully believe you're being true.
—HASNA HASSAN SIRAJEDDINE

1 People have the strength to overcome their bodies. Their beauty is in their minds.

—PETER GABRIEL CLARK-BROWN
in *Style* magazine

2 It is amazing how complete is the delusion that beauty is goodness.

—LEO TOLSTOY

3 I'm tired of all this nonsense about beauty being only skin-deep. That's deep enough. What do you want—an adorable pancreas?

—JEAN KERR
The Snake Has All the Lines

4 Nothing makes a woman more beautiful than the belief that she is beautiful.

—SOPHIA LOREN
Women & Beauty

5 Fashions fade; style is eternal.

—YVES SAINT LAURENT

6 The most beautiful thing we can experience is the mysterious. It is the source of all true art and science.

—ALBERT EINSTEIN

SPEAK THE TRUTH . . .

7 Speak the truth, but leave immediately after.

—SLOVENIAN PROVERB

8 Never assume the obvious is true.

—WILLIAM SAFIRE
Sleeper Spy

9 I have one request: may I never use my reason against truth.

—ELIE WIESEL
quoting from a Hasidic rabbi's prayer

10 Truth isn't always beauty, but the hunger for it is.

—NADINE GORDIMER

11 The truth is not always dressed for the evening.

—MARGARET LEWERTH
Stuyvesant Square

12 Truth has no special time of its own. Its hour is now—always.

—ALBERT SCHWEITZER
On the Edge of the Primeval Forest

13 Only the truth can still astonish people.

—JEAN-MARIE POUPART
Ma Tite Vache A Mal Aux Pattes

14 Some people so treasure the truth that they use it with great economy.

—H. RAY GOLENOR

15 A half truth is a whole lie.

—YIDDISH PROVERB

16 A half-truth is usually less than half of that.

—BERN WILLIAMS

1 A truth that's told with bad intent
beats all the lies you can invent.
—WILLIAM BLAKE

2 The most dangerous untruths are
truths moderately distorted.
—GEORG CHRISTOPH LICHTENBERG

3 Add one small bit to the truth and
you inevitably subtract from it.
—*Dell Crossword Puzzles*

4 Many people today don't want
honest answers insofar as honest
means unpleasant or disturbing.
They want a soft answer that
turneth away anxiety.
—LOUIS KRONENBERGER

5 The man who is brutally honest
enjoys the brutality quite as much
as the honesty. Possibly more.
—RICHARD J. NEEDHAM
in *The Globe and Mail* (Toronto)

6 We have to live today by what
truth we can get today and
be ready tomorrow to call it
falsehood.
—WILLIAM JAMES

7 Truth is tough. It will not break,
like a bubble, at a touch. Nay,
you may kick it about all day,
and it will be round and
full at evening.
—OLIVER WENDELL HOLMES SR.

8 Most of the change we think we
see in life is due to truths being in
and out of favor.
—ROBERT FROST

9 Truth hurts—not the searching
after; the running from!
—JOHN EYBERG

10 The truth will ouch.
—ARNOLD H. GLASOW

11 Of course, it's the same old
story. Truth usually is the same
old story.
—MARGARET THATCHER

12 The color of truth is gray.
—ANDRÉ GIDE

13 One of the most striking differences between a cat and a lie is
that a cat has only nine lives.
—MARK TWAIN

14 A lie has speed, but truth has
endurance.
—EDGAR J. MOHN

15 Every time you try to smother a
truth, two others get their breath.
—BILL COPELAND

16 What upsets me is not that you
lied to me, but that from now on
I can no longer believe you.
—FRIEDRICH NIETZSCHE

1 He who mistrusts most should be trusted least.

—THEOGNIS

2 I seem to have been like a child playing on the sea shore, finding now and then a prettier shell than ordinary, whilst the great ocean of truth lay undiscovered before me.

—ISAAC NEWTON

3 A paradox is a truth that bites its own tale.

—*American Farm & Home Almanac*

4 We always weaken whatever we exaggerate.

—JEAN-FRANÇOISE DE LA HARPE

5 Nothing lays itself open to the charge of exaggeration more than the language of naked truth.

—JOSEPH CONRAD

6 Always tell the truth. You may make a hole in one when you're alone on the golf course someday.

—FRANKLIN P. JONES

7 It takes two to speak truth—one to speak and another to hear.

—HENRY DAVID THOREAU

8 We do not err because truth is difficult to see. It is visible at a glance. We err because this is more comfortable.

—ALEXANDER SOLZHENITSYN

9 We lie loudest when we lie to ourselves.

—ERIC HOFFER

10 Men hate those to whom they have to lie.

—VICTOR HUGO

11 The most exhausting thing in life is being insincere.

—ANNE MORROW LINDBERGH
Gift from the Sea

12 When you stretch the truth, watch out for the snapback.

—BILL COPELAND

HAPPINESS LIES IN WAIT . . .

13 Happiness lies in wait; it comes upon suddenly, like a midnight thief at a turn up in the street, or in the midst of a dream, because a ray of light, a strain of music, a face, or a gesture has overcome the despair of living.

—HECTOR BIANCIOTTI
Sans la Misericorde du Christ

14 Happiness walks on busy feet.

—KITTE TURMELL

15 If only we'd stop trying to be happy, we could have a pretty good time.

—WILLARD R. ESPY

1 Man must search for what is right, and let happiness come on its own.

—Johann Pestalozzi

2 Now and then it's good to pause in our pursuit of happiness and just be happy.

—Quoted in *The Cockle Bur*

3 To be without some of the things you want is an indispensable part of happiness.

—Bertrand Russell
The Conquest of Happiness

4 Before strongly desiring anything, we should look carefully into the happiness of its present owner.

—François de La Rochefoucauld

5 It is an illusion to think that more comfort means more happiness. Happiness comes of the capacity to feel deeply, to enjoy simply, to think freely, to be needed.

—Storm Jameson

6 Happiness is a way station between too little and too much.

—Channing Pollock
Mr. Moneypenny

7 Most people ask for happiness on condition. Happiness can be felt only if you don't set any conditions.

—Arthur Rubinstein

8 Most men pursue pleasure with such breathless haste that they hurry past it.

—Soren Kierkegaard

9 The foolish person seeks happiness in the distance; the wise person grows it under his feet.

—James Oppenheim

10 Fortify yourself with contentment, for this is an impregnable fortress.

—Epictetus

11 The discontented man finds no easy chair.

—Benjamin Franklin

12 Real elation is when you feel you could touch a star without standing on tiptoe.

—Doug Larson

13 The more the heart is nourished with happiness, the more it is insatiable.

—Gabrielle Roy

14 Joy seems to me a step beyond happiness—happiness is a sort of atmosphere you can live in sometimes when you're lucky. Joy is a light that fills you with hope and faith and love.

—Adela Rogers St. Johns
Some Are Born Great

1 Happiness is good health and a bad memory.

—INGRID BERGMAN

2 The summit of happiness is reached when a person is ready to be what he is.

—ERASMUS

3 Don't wait around for other people to be happy for you. Any happiness you get you've got to make yourself.

—ALICE WALKER

4 Happiness is a thing to be practiced, like the violin.

—JOHN LUBBOCK

5 One filled with joy preaches without preaching.

—MOTHER TERESA OF CALCUTTA

6 Happiness is a conscious choice, not an automatic response.

—MILDRED BARTHEL
in *Ensign*

7 Happiness often sneaks in through a door you didn't know you left open.

—JOHN BARRYMORE

8 To show a child what once delighted you, to find the child's delight added to your own—this is happiness.

—J. B. PRIESTLEY

9 There can be no happiness if the things we believe in are different from the things we do.

—FREYA STARK
The Journey's Echo

10 Shared joy is double joy and shared sorrow is half-sorrow.

—SWEDISH PROVERB

11 Success is getting what you want. Happiness is liking what you get.

—H. JACKSON BROWN
A Father's Book of Wisdom

12 An ecstasy is a thing that will not go into words; it feels like music.

—MARK TWAIN

13 Great joys, like griefs, are silent.

—SHACKERLEY MARMION

14 For happiness one needs security, but joy can spring like a flower even from the cliffs of despair.

—ANNE MORROW LINDBERGH

15 If you want others to be happy, practice compassion. If you want to be happy, practice compassion.

—DALAI LAMA

16 Unhappiness is the ultimate form of self-indulgence.

—TOM ROBBINS
Jitterbug Perfume

HUMOR IS NOT A TRICK . . .

1 Humor is not a trick, not jokes. Humor is a presence in the world—like grace—and shines on everybody.

—GARRISON KEILLOR

2 Time spent laughing is time spent with the gods.

—JAPANESE PROVERB

3 Laughter is the shortest distance between two people.

—VICTOR BORGE

4 Laughter is the sun that drives winter from the human face.

—VICTOR HUGO

5 Laughter is a tranquilizer with no side effects.

—ARNOLD H. GLASOW

6 Like a welcome summer rain, humor may suddenly cleanse and cool the earth, the air and you.

—LANGSTON HUGHES
The Book of Negro Humor

7 Laughter is the brush that sweeps away the cobwebs of the heart.

—MORT WALKER

8 Laughter can be heard farther than weeping.

—YIDDISH PROVERB

9 Laughter translates into any language.

—*Graffiti*

10 The kind of humor I like is the thing that makes me laugh for five seconds and think for ten minutes.

—WILLIAM DAVIS

11 Good humor may be said to be one of the very best articles of dress one can wear in society.

—WILLIAM MAKEPEACE THACKERAY

12 Among those whom I like, I can find no common denominator; but among those whom I love, I can: all of them make me laugh.

—W. H. AUDEN

13 After God created the world, He made man and woman. Then, to keep the whole thing from collapsing, He invented humor.

—GUILLERMO MORDILLO

14 Imagination was given to man to compensate him for what he is not; a sense of humor, to console him for what he is.

—*The Wall Street Journal*

15 So many tangles in life are ultimately hopeless that we have no appropriate sword other than laughter.

—GORDON W. ALLPORT

1 Wit surprises, humor illuminates.
—ELI SCHLEIFER

2 It always hurts a bit when you strike your funny bone. That's the essence of humor.
—JIM FIEBIG

3 Someone who makes you laugh is a comedian. Someone who makes you think and then laugh is a humorist.
—GEORGE BURNS

4 We do have a zeal for laughter in most situations, give or take a dentist.
—JOSEPH HELLER

5 Nothing makes your sense of humor disappear faster than having somebody ask where it is.
—IVERN BALL
in *The Saturday Evening Post*

6 If you're going to be able to look back on something and laugh about it, you might as well laugh about it now.
—MARIE OSMOND

7 Anyone without a sense of humor is at the mercy of everyone else.
—WILLIAM ROTSLER

8 Beware of those who laugh at nothing or at everything.
—ARNOLD H. GLASOW

Next to power without honor, the most dangerous thing in the world is power without humor. 9
—ERIC SEVAREID

The love of truth lies at the root of much humor. 10
ROBERTSON DAVIES
in *Our Living Tradition*

I think the next best thing to solving a problem is finding some humor in it. 11
—FRANK A. CLARK

Humor is a hole that lets the sawdust out of a stuffed shirt. 12
—JAN MCKEITHEN

Humor is laughing at what you haven't got when you ought to have it. 13
—LANGSTON HUGHES

A humorist is a fellow who realizes, first, that he is no better than anybody else, and, second, that nobody else is either. 14
—HOMER MCLIN

Comedy has to be based on truth. You take the truth and you put a little curlicue at the end. 15
—SID CAESAR

Comedy is simply a funny way of being serious. 16
—PETER USTINOV

1 Always laugh at yourself first—
before others do.

—ELSA MAXWELL
R.S.V.P.: Elsa Maxwell's Own Story

2 A laugh at your own expense
costs you nothing.

—MARY H. WALDRIP
in *Advertiser* (Dawson County, Georgia)

3 Happy is the person who can
laugh at himself. He will never
cease to be amused.

—HABIB BOURGUIBA

4 Humor is a spontaneous, wonderful bit of an outburst that just
comes. It's unbridled, it's
unplanned, it's full of surprises.

—ERMA BOMBECK

5 Humor is a reminder that no matter how high the throne one sits
on, one sits on one's bottom.

—TAKI

6 You cannot hold back a good
laugh any more than you can the
tide. Both are forces of nature.

—WILLIAM ROTSLER

7 It has always seemed to me that
hearty laughter is a good way to
jog internally without having to go
outdoors.

—NORMAN COUSINS
Anatomy of an Illness

8 When the first baby laughed for
the first time, the laugh broke into
a thousand pieces and they all
went skipping about, and that was
the beginning of fairies.

—JAMES M. BARRIE

9 No symphony orchestra ever
played music like a two-year-old
girl laughing with a puppy.

—BERN WILLIAMS
in *National Enquirer*

10 A pun is the lowest form of
humor, unless you thought of it
yourself.

—DOUG LARSON

WIT OUGHT TO BE A GLORIOUS TREAT . . .

11 Wit ought to be a glorious treat,
like caviar. Never spread it about
like marmalade.

—NOËL COWARD

12 Wit has truth in it; wisecracking is
simply calisthenics with words.

—DOROTHY PARKER
in *The Paris Review*

13 Wit is the salt of conversation, not
the food.

—WILLIAM HAZLITT

14 Wit is educated insolence.

—ARISTOTLE

1 A caricature is always true only
for an instant.
—CHRISTIAN MORGENSTERN

2 Wit penetrates; humor envelops.
Wit is a function of verbal intelli-
gence; humor is imagination
operating on good nature.
—PEGGY NOONAN
What I Saw at the Revolution

3 The wit of conversation consists
more in finding it in others than
in showing a great deal yourself.
—JEAN DE LA BRUYÈRE

THE ONLY WAY TO KEEP
YOUR HEALTH . . .

4 The only way to keep your health
is to eat what you don't want,
drink what you don't like, and
do what you'd druther not.
—MARK TWAIN

5 The only way for a rich man to be
healthy is, by exercise and absti-
nence, to live as if he were poor.
—PAUL DUDLEY WHITE

6 So many people spend their
health gaining wealth, and then
have to spend their wealth to
regain their health.
—A. J. REB MATERI
Our Family

7 It would be a service to mankind
if the pill were available in slot
machines and the cigarette were
placed on prescription.
—MALCOLM POTTS, MD
in *The Observer* (London)

8 The best cure for hypochondria is
to forget about your own body
and get interested in someone
else's.
—GOODMAN ACE

9 Those who think they have not
time for bodily exercise will
sooner or later have to find time
for illness.
—EDWARD STANLEY

10 It is part of the cure to wish to be
cured.
—SENECA

11 You know you've reached middle
age when a doctor, not a policeman, tells you to slow down, all
you exercise are your prerogatives
and it takes you longer to rest
than to get tired.
—*Friends News Sheet*
(Royal Perth Hospital, Australia)

12 An early-morning walk is a blessing
for the whole day.
—HENRY DAVID THOREAU

13 As with liberty, the price of
leanness is eternal vigilance.
—GENE BROWN

1 Your body is the baggage you must carry through life. The more excess baggage, the shorter the trip.

—ARNOLD H. GLASOW

2 You can't lose weight by talking about it. You have to keep your mouth shut.

—*The Old Farmers Almanac*

3 You know it's time to diet when you push away from the table and the table moves.

—Quoted in *The Cockle Bur*

4 Probably nothing in the world arouses more false hopes than the first four hours of a diet.

—DAN BENNETT

5 If it weren't for the fact that the TV set and the refrigerator are so far apart, some of us wouldn't get any exercise at all.

—JOEY ADAMS

TAKING MY PROBLEMS ONE AT A TIME . . .

6 It's not easy taking my problems one at a time when they refuse to get in line.

—ASHLEIGH BRILLIANT

7 He who can't endure the bad will not live to see the good.

—YIDDISH PROVERB

8 It has been my philosophy of life that difficulties vanish when faced boldly.

—ISAAC ASIMOV
Foundation

9 When things are bad, we take comfort in the thought that they could always be worse. And when they are, we find hope in the thought that things are so bad they have to get better.

—MALCOLM S. FORBES
The Sayings of Chairman Malcolm

10 I don't think of all the misery but of the beauty that still remains.

—ANNE FRANK
The Diary of a Young Girl

11 Although the world is full of suffering, it is also full of the overcoming of it.

—HELEN KELLER

12 Nothing is more desirable than to be released from an affliction, but nothing is more frightening than to be divested of a crutch.

—JAMES BALDWIN

13 A certain amount of opposition is a great help to a man. Kites rise against, not with, the wind.

—JOHN NEAL

14 What I'm looking for is a blessing that's not in disguise.

—KITTY O'NEILL COLLINS

1 People need resistance, for it is resistance which gives them their awareness of life.

—KARL RITTER

2 That some good can be derived from every event is a better proposition than that everything happens for the best, which it assuredly does not.

—JAMES K. FEIBLEMAN

3 The worst thing in your life may contain seeds of the best. When you can see crisis as an opportunity, your life becomes not easier, but more satisfying.

—JOE KOGEL

4 Storms make trees take deeper roots.

—CLAUDE MCDONALD
in *The Christian Word*

5 Smooth seas do not make skillful sailors.

—AFRICAN PROVERB

6 It is the wounded oyster that mends its shell with pearl.

—RALPH WALDO EMERSON

7 The soul would have no rainbow had the eyes no tears.

—JOHN VANCE CHENEY

8 Some people are always grumbling that roses have thorns; I am thankful that thorns have roses.

—ALPHONSE KARR

9 He knows not his own strength that hath not met adversity.

—BEN JONSON

10 Adversity is the trial of principle. Without it, a man hardly knows whether he is honest or not.

—HENRY FIELDING

11 You'll never find a better sparring partner than adversity.

—WALT SCHMIDT
in *Parklabrea News* (Los Angeles)

12 A gem is not polished without rubbing, nor a man perfected without trials.

—CHINESE PROVERB

13 Drag your thoughts away from your troubles—by the ears, by the heels, or any other way you can manage it. It's the healthiest thing a body can do.

—MARK TWAIN

14 Borrow trouble for yourself if that's your nature, but don't lend it to your neighbors.

—RUDYARD KIPLING
Rewards and Fairies

15 Don't meet trouble halfway. It is quite capable of making the entire journey.

—BOB EDWARDS

16 Simple solutions seldom are.

—*Forbes* magazine

1 No one has completed his education who has not learned to live with an insoluble problem.
—EDMUND J. KIEFER

2 Keep your face to the sunshine and you cannot see the shadows.
—HELEN KELLER

3 When you can't solve the problem, manage it.
—REV. ROBERT H. SCHULLER

4 Most problems precisely defined are already partially solved.
—HARRY LORAYNE
Memory Makes Money

5 If the only tool you have is a hammer, you tend to see every problem as a nail.
—ABRAHAM MASLOW

6 Nothing lasts forever—not even your troubles.
—ARNOLD H. GLASOW
in *Rotary "Scandal Sheet"* (Graham, Texas)

7 People who drink to drown their sorrow should be told that sorrow knows how to swim.
—ANN LANDERS

8 The way I see it, if you want the rainbow, you gotta put up with the rain.
—DOLLY PARTON

9 The human capacity to fight back will always astonish doctors and philosophers. It seems, indeed, that there are no circumstances so bad and no obstacles so big that man cannot conquer them.
—JEAN TETREAU

10 How a person masters his fate is more important than what his fate is.
—WILHELM VON HUMBOLDT

11 All blessings are mixed blessings.
—JOHN UPDIKE

12 Most of the shadows of this life are caused by our standing in our own sunshine.
—RALPH WALDO EMERSON

13 Life would not be life if a sorrow were sad, and a joy merry, from beginning to end.
—GERMAINE GUEVREMONT
EN PLEINE TERRE

14 Night is the blotting paper for many sorrows.
—LITAUISCH

15 The darkest hour has only 60 minutes.
—MORRIS MANDEL

16 When you get to the end of your rope, tie a knot and hang on. And swing!
—LEO BUSCAGLIA

1 Every problem contains within itself the seeds of its own solution.
—EDWARD SOMERS
in *National Enquirer*

2 Worry often gives a small thing a big shadow.
—SWEDISH PROVERB

3 Little things console us because little things afflict us.
—BLAISE PASCAL

4 For every problem there is one solution which is simple, neat and wrong.
—H. L. MENCKEN
A Mencken Chrestomathy

5 Inside every small problem is a large problem struggling to get out.
—PAUL HUGHES

6 People in distress will sometimes prefer a problem that is familiar to a solution that is not.
—NEIL POSTMAN

7 The first step in solving a problem is to tell someone about it.
—JOHN PETER FLYNN

8 Some people suffer in silence louder than others.
—MORRIE BRICKMAN

Untold suffering seldom is. 9
—FRANKLIN P. JONES

Never bear more than one kind of 10 trouble at a time. Some people bear three—all they have had, all they have now, and all they expect to have.
—EDWARD EVERETT HALE

An adventure is an inconvenience 11 rightly considered. An inconvenience is an adventure wrongly considered.
—G. K. CHESTERTON

IT IS THE LOOSE ENDS . . .

It is the loose ends with which 12 men hang themselves.
—ZELDA FITZGERALD

Two dangers constantly threaten 13 the world: order and disorder.
—PAUL VALÉRY

Nothing is really lost. It's just 14 where it doesn't belong.
—SUZANNE MUELLER

One of the advantages of being 15 disorderly is that one is constantly making exciting discoveries.
—A. A. MILNE

More things grow in the garden 16 than the gardener sows.
—SPANISH PROVERB

1 Organizing is what you do before you do something, so that when you do it, it's not all mixed up.
—A. A. MILNE

2 When one finds himself in a hole of his own making, it is a good time to examine the quality of workmanship.
—JON REMMERDE
in *The Christian Science Monitor*

WHEN LUCK ENTERS . . .

3 When luck enters, give him a seat!
—JEWISH PROVERB

4 A person often meets his destiny on the road he took to avoid it.
—JEAN DE LA FONTAINE

5 Fortune brings in some boats that are not steered.
—WILLIAM SHAKESPEARE

6 Heaven goes by favor. If it went by merit, you would stay out and your dog would go in.
—MARK TWAIN

7 It's hard to detect good luck—it looks so much like something you've earned.
—FRANK A. CLARK

8 Luck is the residue of design.
—BRANCH RICKEY

9 The luck of having talent is not enough; one must also have a talent for luck.
—HECTOR BERLIOZ

10 Luck never gives; it only lends.
—SWEDISH PROVERB

11 Good luck is with the man who doesn't include it in his plan.
—*Graffiti*

12 Thorough preparation makes its own luck.
—JOE POYER
The Contra

13 Luck is a matter of preparation meeting opportunity.
—OPRAH WINFREY

14 Miracles sometimes occur, but one has to work terribly hard for them.
—CHAIM WEIZMANN

15 Luck is not chance, it's toil. Fortune's expensive smile is earned.
—EMILY DICKINSON

16 One half of life is luck; the other half is discipline—and that's the important half, for without discipline you wouldn't know what to do with your luck.
—CARL ZUCKMAYER

1 With money in your pocket, you
are wise and you are handsome
and you sing well, too.
—YIDDISH PROVERB

2 Some people have all the luck.
And they're the ones who never
depend on it.
—BOB INGHAM

3 There is no substitute for incom-
prehensible good luck.
—LYNNE ALPERN AND ESTHER BLUMENFELD
Oh, Lord, I Sound Just Like Mama

4 Serendipity is looking in a
haystack for a needle and discovering the farmer's daughter.
—Quoted by JULIUS H. COMROE JR.
in *Retrospectroscope*

5 It is an all-too-human frailty to
suppose that a favorable wind will
blow forever.
—RICK BODE
First You Have to Row a Little Boat

6 It is perhaps a more fortunate
destiny to have a taste for
collecting shells than to be born
a millionaire.
—ROBERT LOUIS STEVENSON

7 Superstition is foolish, childish,
primitive and irrational—but how
much does it cost you to knock
on wood?
—JUDITH VIORST
Love & Guilt & the Meaning of Life, Etc.

THE LIMITS OF THE POSSIBLE . . .

The only way of discovering the
limits of the possible is to venture
a little way past them into the
impossible. 8
—ARTHUR C. CLARKE
Profiles of the Future

I have learned to use the word
impossible with the greatest
caution. 9
—WERNHER VON BRAUN

What we need are more people
who specialize in the impossible. 10
—THEODORE ROETHKE

The difference between the
impossible and the possible lies
in a person's determination. 11
—TOMMY LASORDA

The impossible is often the untried. 12
—JIM GOODWIN

All things are possible until they
are proved impossible—and even
the impossible may only be so,
as of now. 13
—PEARL S. BUCK
A Bridge for Passing

Progress begins with the belief
that what is necessary is possible. 14
—NORMAN COUSINS

1 Start by doing what's necessary, then what's possible and suddenly you are doing the impossible.

—St. Francis of Assisi

2 Everything looks impossible for the people who never try anything.

—Jean-Louis Etienne

3 The young do not know enough to be prudent, and therefore they attempt the impossible—and achieve it, generation after generation.

—Pearl S. Buck

4 Nothing ever built arose to touch the skies unless some man dreamed that it should, some man believed that it could, and some man willed that it must.

—Charles F. Kettering

5 Accomplishing the impossible means only that the boss will add it to your regular duties.

—Doug Larson

IF YOU WANT A PLACE IN THE SUN . . .

6 If you want a place in the sun, you've got to put up with a few blisters.

—Abigail Van Buren

7 Always bear in mind that your own resolution to succeed is more important than any one thing.

—Abraham Lincoln

8 Probably the most honest "self-made man" ever was the one we heard say: "I got to the top the hard way—fighting my own laziness and ignorance every step of the way."

—James Thom

9 You can't expect to make a place in the sun for yourself if you keep taking refuge under the family tree.

—Claude McDonald
in The Christian Word

10 The important thing in life is not to have a good hand but to play it well.

—Louis-N. Fortin
Pensées, Proverbes, Maximes

11 Striving for success without hard work is like trying to harvest where you haven't planted.

—David Bly
in Deseret News (Salt Lake City)

12 Showing up is 80 percent of life.

—Woody Allen

13 If you play to win, as I do, the game never ends.

—Stan Mikita
Journal (Edmonton, Alberta)

1 There are no secrets to success. It is the result of preparation, hard work, learning from failure.
—GEN. COLIN L. POWELL
in *The Black Collegian*

2 Success is how high you bounce when you hit bottom.
—GEN. GEORGE S. PATTON

3 Success is often the result of taking a misstep in the right direction.
—AL BERNSTEIN

4 Wherever you see a successful business, someone once made a courageous decision.
—PETER DRUCKER

5 Success is often just an idea away.
—FRANK TYGER

6 The only thing that ever sat its way to success was a hen.
—SARAH BROWN

7 Success has a simple formula: do your best, and people may like it.
—SAM EWING

8 As a general rule, the most successful man in life is the man who has the best information.
—BENJAMIN DISRAELI

9 You're never a loser until you quit trying.
—MIKE DITKA

10 There's no secret about success. Did you ever know a successful man who didn't tell you about it?
—KIN HUBBARD

11 Success is more a function of consistent common sense than it is of genius.
—AN WANG
Lessons: An Autobiography

12 Don't aim for success if you want it; just do what you love and believe in, and it will come naturally.
—DAVID FROST

13 Success isn't a result of spontaneous combustion. You must set yourself on fire.
—ARNOLD H. GLASOW

14 Success without honor is an unseasoned dish; it will satisfy your hunger, but it won't taste good.
—JOE PATERNO

15 Sports serve society by providing vivid examples of excellence.
—GEORGE F. WILL

16 Always do what you say you are going to do. It is the glue and fiber that binds successful relationships.
—JEFFRY A. TIMMONS
The Entrepreneurial Mind

THE NATURAL WORLD

When one tugs at a single thing in nature,
he finds it attached to the rest of the world.
—JOHN MUIR

A FINE LANDSCAPE IS LIKE A PIECE OF MUSIC . . .

1 There is nothing like walking to get the feel of a country. A fine landscape is like a piece of music; it must be taken at the right tempo. Even a bicycle goes too fast.

—PAUL SCOTT MOWRER
The House of Europe

2 When one tugs at a single thing in nature, he finds it attached to the rest of the world.

—JOHN MUIR

3 The universe is not required to be in perfect harmony with human ambition.

—CARL SAGAN

4 Our Creator would never have made such lovely days and have given us the deep hearts to enjoy them unless we were meant to be immortal.

—NATHANIEL HAWTHORNE

5 Climb the mountains and get their good tidings. Nature's peace will flow into you as sunshine flows into trees. The winds will blow their freshness into you, and the storms their energy, while cares will drop off like falling leaves.

—JOHN MUIR

6 There is no silence like that of the mountains.

—GUY BUTLER
A Local Habitation

7 I have seen the sea when it is stormy and wild; when it is quiet and serene; when it is dark and moody. And in all its moods, I see myself.

—MARTIN BUXBAUM

8 April hath put a spirit of youth in every thing.

—WILLIAM SHAKESPEARE

9 Our Lord has written the promise of resurrection, not in books alone but in every leaf of springtime.

—MARTIN LUTHER

10 Spring hangs her infant blossoms on the trees / Rock'd in the cradle of the western breeze.

—WILLIAM COWPER

11 Spring, thy name is color.

—LIBBIE FUDIM

12 Spring is nature's way of saying, "Let's party!"

—ROBIN WILLIAMS

13 A little madness in the spring is wholesome even for the king.

—EMILY DICKINSON

1 Springtime is the land awakening. The March winds are the morning yawn.
—Quoted by Lewis Grizzard
in *Kathy Sue Loudermilk, I Love You*

2 The first day of spring is one thing, and the first spring day is another. The difference between them is sometimes as great as a month.
—HENRY VAN DYKE

3 Spring is when you feel like whistling even with a shoe full of slush.
—DOUG LARSON

4 Summer afternoon—summer afternoon; to me those have always been the two most beautiful words in the English language.
—HENRY JAMES

5 If a June night could talk, it would probably boast that it invented romance.
—BERN WILLIAMS

6 Until you have heard the whippoorwill, either nearby or in the faint distance, you have not experienced summer night.
—HENRY BEETLE HOUGH
in *Vineyard Gazette* (Edgartown, Massachusetts)

Oh, the summer night has a smile 7 of light, and she sits on a sapphire throne.
—B. W. PROCTER

The experience of drought and 8 dust storms remains central to the psychology of the prairie west; more than the intermittent affluence of postwar decades, it tints a westerner's outlook on life. He continues to live in next year country, where he smokes a pack of hope a day.
—MARK ABLEY
Beyond Forget

For man, autumn is a time of 9 harvest, of gathering together. For nature, it is a time of sowing, of scattering abroad.
—EDWIN WAY TEALE
Autumn Across America

Autumn is a second spring when 10 every leaf is a flower.
—ALBERT CAMUS

Autumn carries more gold in its 11 hand than all the other seasons.
—JIM BISHOP

October's poplars are flaming 12 torches lighting the way to winter.
—NOVA S. BAIR
in *Capper's Weekly*

1 October, here's to you. Here's to the heady aroma of the frost-kissed apples, the winey smell of ripened grapes, the wild-as-the-wind smell of hickory nuts and the nostalgic whiff of that first wood smoke.

—KEN WEBER
in Providence, R.I., *Journal-Bulletin*

2 Autumn is a season followed immediately by looking forward to spring.

—DOUG LARSON

3 Winter is not a season; it's an occupation.

—SINCLAIR LEWIS

4 Few things are as democratic as a snowstorm.

—BERN WILLIAMS
in *The National Enquirer*

5 No winter lasts forever; no spring skips its turn.

—HAL BORLAND
Sundial of the Seasons

6 All sunshine makes a desert.

—ARABIC PROVERB

7 I am sure it is a great mistake always to know enough to go in when it rains. One may keep snug and dry by such knowledge, but one misses a world of loveliness.

—ADELINE KNAPP

8 When there is a river in your growing up, you probably always hear it.

—ANN ZWINGER
Run, River, Run

9 I like trees because they seem more resigned to the way they have to live than other things do.

—WILLA CATHER

10 A man has made at least a start on discovering the meaning of human life when he plants shade trees under which he knows full well he will never sit.

—D. ELTON TRUEBLOOD

11 I never knew how soothing trees are—many trees and patches of open sunlight, and tree presences; it is almost like having another being.

—D. H. LAWRENCE

12 The soil in return for her service keeps the tree tied to her, the sky asks nothing and leaves it free.

—RABINDRANATH TAGORE

13 Everything is blooming most recklessly; if it were voices instead of colors, there would be an unbelievable shrieking into the heart of the night.

—RAINER MARIA RILKE
Letters of Rainer Maria Rilke

1 A woodland in full color is awesome as a forest fire; but a single tree is like a dancing tongue of flame to warm the heart.

—HAL BORLAND
Sundial of the Seasons

2 He that plants trees loves others besides himself.

—ENGLISH PROVERB

3 Flowers always make people better, happier and more helpful; they are sunshine, food and medicine to the soul.

—LUTHER BURBANK

4 If we had a keen vision of all that is ordinary in human life, it would be like hearing the grass grow or the squirrel's heart beat, and we should die of that roar which is the other side of silence.

—GEORGE ELIOT

5 People from a planet without flowers would think we must be mad with joy the whole time to have such things about us.

—IRIS MURDOCH
A Fairly Honourable Defeat

6 The Pyramids will not last a moment compared with the daisy.

—D. H. LAWRENCE
D. H. Lawrence and Italy

7 I don't see why I am always asking for private, individual, selfish miracles when every year there are miracles like white dogwood.

—ANNE MORROW LINDBERGH
Bring Me a Unicorn

8 I don't ask for the meaning of the song of a bird or the rising of the sun on a misty morning. There they are, and they are beautiful.

—PETE HAMILL
in *Esquire*

9 A bird does not sing because it has an answer. It sings because it has a song.

—CHINESE PROVERB

10 Let us a little permit nature to take her own way; she better understands her own affairs than we.

—MONTAIGNE

11 I've always regarded nature as the clothing of God.

—ALAN HOVHANESS

12 The sky is the daily bread of the eyes.

—RALPH WALDO EMERSON

13 One touch of nature makes the whole world kin.

—WILLIAM SHAKESPEARE

14 Repetition is the only form of permanence that nature can achieve.

—GEORGE SANTAYANA

1 The repetition in nature may not be a mere recurrence. It may be a theatrical "encore."
—G. K. Chesterton

2 Everybody wants to go back to nature—but not on foot.
—Werner Mitsch

3 Never a daisy grows but a mystery guides the growing.
—Richard Realf

4 I would rather live in a world where my life is surrounded by mystery than live in a world so small that my mind could comprehend it.
—Harry Emerson Fosdick

5 If the human brain were so simple that we could understand it, we would be so simple that we couldn't.
—Emerson M. Pugh

6 Science cannot answer the deepest questions. As soon as you ask why there is something instead of nothing, you have gone beyond science. I find it quite improbable that such order came out of chaos. There has to be some organizing principle. God to me is the explanation for the miracle of existence—why there is something instead of nothing.
—Cosmologist Allan R. Sandage

7 Sometimes I think we're alone in the universe, and sometimes I think we're not. In either case, the idea is quite staggering.
—Arthur C. Clarke

8 Unknowingly, we plow the dust of stars, blown about us by the wind, and drink the universe in a glass of rain.
—Ihab Hassan

9 The universe is full of magical things patiently waiting for our wits to grow sharper.
—Eden Phillpotts
A Shadow Passes

10 The sun, with all those planets revolving around it and dependent on it, can still ripen a bunch of grapes as if it had nothing else in the universe to do.
—Galileo

11 To define the universe would be to contain it, and that would be to limit existence.
—David Beresford
in The Weekly Mail & Guardian
(Johannesburg, South Africa)

12 The universe is merely a fleeting idea in God's mind—a pretty uncomfortable thought, particularly if you've just made a down payment on a house.
—Woody Allen

LEAVE A LANDSCAPE AS IT WAS . . .

1 There is nothing in which the birds differ more from man than the way in which they can build and yet leave a landscape as it was before.

—ROBERT LYND
The Blue Lion and Other Essays

2 Don't blow it—good planets are hard to find.

—Quoted in *Time*

3 What is the use of a house if you haven't got a tolerable planet to put it on?

—HENRY DAVID THOREAU

4 It is horrifying that we have to fight our own government to save the environment.

—ANSEL ADAMS

5 Growth for the sake of growth is the ideology of the cancer cell.

—EDWARD ABBEY

6 Progress might have been all right once, but it's gone on too long.

—OGDEN NASH

7 Progress is man's ability to complicate simplicity.

—THOR HEYERDAHL
Fatu-Hiva

8 You can tell all you need to about a society from how it treats animals and beaches.

—FRANK DEFORD
in *Sports Illustrated*

9 Since the beginning each generation has fought nature. Now, in the life-span of a single generation, we must turn around 180 degrees and become the protector of nature.

—JACQUES-YVES COUSTEAU

10 We haven't got too much time left to ensure that government of the earth, by the earth, for the earth, shall not perish from the people.

—C. P. SNOW

11 The activist is not the man who says the river is dirty. The activist is the man who cleans up the river.

—ROSS PEROT

12 I think God's going to come down and pull civilization over for speeding.

—STEVEN WRIGHT

13 Civilization no longer needs to open up wilderness; it needs wilderness to open up the still largely unexplored human mind.

—DAVID RAINS WALLACE
The Dark Range

1 If we do not permit the earth to produce beauty and joy, it will in the end not produce food either.

—Joseph Wood Krutch

2 We abuse land because we regard it as a commodity belonging to us. When we see land as a community to which we belong, we may begin to use it with love and respect.

—Aldo Leopold
A Sand County Almanac

3 A true conservationist is a man who knows that the world is not given by his fathers but borrowed from his children.

—*Audubon*

4 The other planets may not be able to support life, but it isn't easy on this one either.

—*Banking*

THERE'S NO DEALING WITH A CAT . . .

5 There's no dealing with a cat who knows you're awake.

—Brad Solomon
The Open Shadow

6 The only mystery about the cat is why it ever decided to become a domestic animal.

—Compton MacKenzie
Cats' Company

7 The cat could very well be man's best friend but would never stoop to admitting it.

—Doug Larson

8 Cats have it all—admiration and an endless sleep and company only when they want it.

—Rod McKuen
Book of Days

9 Cats don't caress us—they caress themselves on us.

—Rivarol

10 When dogs leap onto your bed, it's because they adore being with you. When cats leap onto your bed, it's because they adore your bed.

—Alisha Everett

11 You can keep a dog; but it is the cat who keeps people because cats find humans useful domestic animals. A dog will flatter you but you have to flatter a cat. A dog is an employee; the cat is a freelance.

—George Mikes
How to Be Decadent

12 When I play with my cat, who knows if I am not more of a pastime to her than she is to me?

—Montaigne

1 Ignorant people think it's the noise which fighting cats make that is so aggravating, but it ain't so; it's the sickening grammar they use.

—MARK TWAIN

2 No matter how much cats fight, there always seem to be plenty of kittens.

—ABRAHAM LINCOLN

3 It is impossible to keep a straight face in the presence of one or more kittens.

—CYNTHIA E. VARNADO

4 You can't look at a sleeping cat and be tense.

—JANE PAULEY

5 The idea of calm exists in a sitting cat.

—JULES RENARD

6 Cats seem to go on the principle that it never does any harm to ask for what you want.

—JOSEPH WOOD KRUTCH
The Twelve Seasons

7 Never try to outstubborn a cat.
—ROBERT A. HEINLEIN
The Notebooks of Lazarus Long

IF DOGS COULD TALK . . .

If dogs could talk, it would take a 8 lot of fun out of owning one.
—ANDREW A. ROONEY
Not That You Asked . . .

One reason a dog can be such a 9 comfort when you're feeling blue is that he doesn't try to find out why.

—*National Enquirer*

There is no psychiatrist in the 10 world like a puppy licking your face.

—BERN WILLIAMS

To his dog, every man is 11 Napoleon; hence the popularity of dogs.

—ALDOUS HUXLEY

The great pleasure of a dog is that 12 you may make a fool of yourself with him and not only will he not scold you, but he will make a fool of himself too.

—SAMUEL BUTLER

The dog has got more fun out of 13 Man than Man has got out of the dog, for the clearly demonstrable reason that Man is the more laughable of the two animals.

—JAMES THURBER
Thurber's Dogs

1 Dogs laugh, but they laugh with their tails.

—MAX EASTMAN
Enjoyment of Laughter

2 A dog wags its tail with its heart.

—MARTIN BUXBAUM
in *Table Talk*

3 A dog teaches a boy fidelity, perseverance, and to turn around three times before lying down.

—ROBERT BENCHLEY

4 Home computers are being called upon to perform many new functions, including the consumption of homework formerly eaten by the dog.

—DOUG LARSON

5 If you think dogs can't count, try putting three dog biscuits in your pocket and then giving Fido only two of them.

—PHIL PASTORET

6 Any time you think you have influence, try ordering around someone else's dog.

—*The Cockle Bur*

7 Door: What a dog is perpetually on the wrong side of.

—OGDEN NASH

8 We give them the love we can spare, the time we can spare. In return dogs have given us their absolute all. It is without a doubt the best deal man has ever made.

—ROGER CARAS
A Celebration of Dogs

THE WORLD OF NATIONS

To understand a man, you must know his memories. The same is true of a nation.

—Anthony Quayle

THE AMERICAN DREAM IS NOT OVER . . .

1 The American dream is not over. America is an adventure.
—THEODORE WHITE

2 There are those who will say that the liberation of humanity, the freedom of man and mind, is nothing but a dream. They are right. It is the American dream.
—ARCHIBALD MACLEISH
A Continuing Journey

3 It is a part of the American character to consider nothing as desperate.
—THOMAS JEFFERSON

4 What is the essence of America? Finding and maintaining that perfect, delicate balance between freedom "to" and freedom "from."
—MARILYN VOS SAVANT
in *Parade*

5 The saving grace of America lies in the fact that the overwhelming majority of Americans are possessed of two great qualities— a sense of humor and a sense of proportion.
—FRANKLIN DELANO ROOSEVELT

6 America is a religious nation, but only because it is religiously tolerant and lets every citizen pray, or not pray, in his own way.
—From an editorial in *The New York Times*

7 America is a place where Jewish merchants sell Zen love beads to agnostics for Christmas.
—JOHN BURTON BRIMER

8 America is great because America is good, and if America ever ceases to be good, America will cease to be great.
—ALEXIS DE TOCQUEVILLE

9 The things that have made America great are being subverted for the things that make Americans rich.
—LOU ERICKSON

10 How often we fail to realize our good fortune in living in a country where happiness is more than a lack of tragedy.
—PAUL SWEENEY

11 America did not invent human rights. In a very real sense, it is the other way around. Human rights invented America.
—JIMMY CARTER

12 What the people want is very simple—they want an America as good as its promise.
—BARBARA JORDAN

1 Being American is not a matter of birth. We must practice it every day, lest we become something else.

—MALCOLM WALLOP
in *Imprimis*

2 What's right with America is a willingness to discuss what's wrong with America.

—HARRY C. BAUER

3 America is not like a blanket—one piece of unbroken cloth. America is more like a quilt—many patches, many pieces, many colors, many sizes, all woven together by a common thread.

—REV. JESSE L. JACKSON

4 America is a tune. It must be sung together.

—GERALD STANLEY LEE
Crowds

5 In America nobody says you have to keep the circumstances somebody else gives you.

—AMY TAN
The Joy Luck Club

6 One of the fondest expressions around is that we can't be the world's policeman. But guess who gets called when suddenly someone needs a cop.

—GEN. COLIN POWELL

7 I thank God that I live in a country where dreams can come true, where failure sometimes is the first step to success and where success is only another form of failure if we forget what our priorities should be.

—HARRY LLOYD

8 Americans are optimists. They hope they'll be wealthy someday—and they're positive they can get one more brushful of paint out of an empty can.

—BERN WILLIAMS

9 Give the American people a good cause, and there's nothing they can't lick.

—JOHN WAYNE

10 The business of America is not business. Neither is it war. The business of America is justice and securing the blessings of liberty.

—GEORGE F. WILL
in *Newsweek*

11 If the American Revolution had produced nothing but the Declaration of Independence, it would have been worthwhile.

—SAMUEL ELIOT MORISON
The Oxford History of the American People

1 Whoever wants to know the heart and mind of America had better learn baseball.

—JACQUES BARZUN
God's Country and Mine

2 Highways have made tangible the conviction that the truth about America, its heart and soul, is always to be found somewhere just over the horizon, somewhere around the next bend.

—PHIL PATTON
Open Road

3 A frontier is never a place; it is a time and a way of life. Frontiers pass, but they endure in their people.

—HAL BORLAND
High, Wide and Lonesome

THE REAL ESSENCE OF CANADA . . .

4 To agree to disagree, to harness diversity, to respect dissent; perhaps this is the real essence of Canada.

—ROBERT L. PERRY
Peter's Quotations

5 The soul of Canada is a dual personality, and must remain only half-revealed to those who know only one language.

—FRANK OLIVER CALL
Canadian Quotations and Phrases

6 A Canadian is someone who drinks Brazilian coffee from an English teacup, and munches a French pastry while sitting on his Danish furniture, having just come home from an Italian movie in his German car. He picks up his Japanese pen and writes to his MP to complain about the American takeover of the Canadian publishing business.

—CAMPBELL HUGHES
in Time

7 "Liberty" sounds awkward on the Canadian tongue; we use "freedom," a more passive-sounding word. When I was a soldier applying for a three-day pass, I asked for "leave," a word that suggests permission. United States G.I.'s were granted "liberty," a word that implies escape.

—PIERRE BERTON
Why We Act Like Canadians

8 Freedom is to you, what the sun was for us. You take it for granted.

—MOHAMED MAGHJI
Vancouver Sun

9 Such a land [British Columbia] is good for an energetic man. It is also not so bad for the loafer.

—RUDYARD KIPLING

LIBERTY IS ALWAYS DANGEROUS . . .

1 Liberty is always dangerous—but it is the safest thing we have.
—HARRY EMERSON FOSDICK

2 Liberty, when it begins to take root, is a plant of rapid growth.
—GEORGE WASHINGTON

3 Let freedom reign. The sun never set on so glorious a human achievement.
—NELSON MANDELA

4 Free is not the same as free and easy.
—LARRY EISENBERG

5 Every generation of Americans needs to know that freedom consists not in doing what we like, but in having the right to do what we ought.
—POPE JOHN PAUL II

6 The cause of freedom, of the defense of man's conscience, is indivisible. By defending it in one country, we defend it everywhere in the world.
—VLADIMIR BUKOVSKY

7 Freedom is the right to be wrong, not the right to do wrong.
—JOHN G. DIEFENBAKER

8 There are two freedoms: the false where a man is free to do what he likes; the true where a man is free to do what he ought.
—CHARLES KINGSLEY

9 Your liberty to swing your arms ends where my nose begins.
—Quoted by STUART CHASE

10 The right to do something does not mean that doing it is right.
—WILLIAM SAFIRE
in *The New York Times*

11 My definition of a free society is a society where it is safe to be unpopular.
—ADLAI E. STEVENSON

12 Many politicians of our time are in the habit of laying down as self-evident the proposition that no people ought to be free until they are fit to use their freedom. The maxim is worthy of the fool in the old story, who had resolved not to go in the water until he had learnt to swim. If men are to wait for liberty until they become wise and good in slavery, they may indeed wait for ever.
—THOMAS BABINGTON MACAULAY, 1825

13 Liberty is the only thing you cannot have unless you are willing to give it to others.
—WILLIAM ALLEN WHITE

1 Freedom is a powerful animal that fights the barriers, and sometimes makes people wish for higher fences.

—LANCE MORROW
in *Time*

2 The function of freedom is to free somebody else.

—TONI MORRISON

3 It is easy to take liberty for granted, when you have never had it taken from you.

—DICK CHENEY

4 Those who expect to reap the blessings of freedom must undergo the fatigue of supporting it.

—THOMAS PAINE

5 Those who profess to favor freedom and yet depreciate agitation are men who want rain without thunder and lightning.

—FREDERICK DOUGLASS

6 Freedom never yet was given to nations as a gift, but only as a reward, bravely earned by one's own exertions.

—LAJOS KOSSUTH

7 The history of liberty is a history of the limitation of government power.

—WOODROW WILSON

They have rights who dare defend 8 them.

—ROGER BALDWIN

The love of liberty is the love of 9 others. The love of power is the love of ourselves.

—WILLIAM HAZLITT

Freedom is nothing else but a 10 chance to be better.

—ALBERT CAMUS
Resistance, Rebellion and Death

Freedom is the right to choose the 11 habits that bind you.

—RENATE RUBENSTEIN
Liefst Verliefd

If a nation values anything more 12 than freedom, it will lose its freedom; and the irony of it is that if it is comfort or money that it values more, it will lose that too.

—W. SOMERSET MAUGHAM,
Strictly Personal

A country free enough to examine 13 its own conscience is a land worth living in, a nation to be envied.

—PRINCE CHARLES

The clash of ideas is the sound of 14 freedom.

—*Graffiti*

1 Where opinions, morals and politics are concerned, there is no such thing as objectivity. The best we can hope for is that freedom will enable subjective points of view to meet and complement each other.

—JEAN D'ORMESSON

2 A people that values its privileges above its principles soon loses both.

—DWIGHT D. EISENHOWER

3 It is a seldom proferred argument as to the advantages of a free press that it has a major function in keeping the government itself informed as to what the government is doing.

—WALTER CRONKITE

4 A free press can be good or bad, but, most certainly, without freedom a press will never be anything but bad.

—ALBERT CAMUS

5 Where the press is free and every man able to read, all is safe.

—THOMAS JEFFERSON

6 Censorship reflects a society's lack of confidence in itself.

—POTTER STEWART

7 Every time we liberate a woman, we liberate a man.

—MARGARET MEAD

8 No man is free who is not master of himself.

—EPICTETUS

9 No woman can call herself free until she can choose consciously whether she will or will not be a mother.

—MARGARET SANGER

10 Freedom always carries a burden of proof, always throws us back on ourselves.

—SHELBY STEELE
The Content of Our Character

11 Patriotism is not so much protecting the land of our fathers as preserving the land of our children.

—JOSÉ ORTEGA Y GASSET

12 If everything would be permitted to me, I would feel lost in this abyss of freedom.

—IGOR STRAVINSKY

13 Freedom is the oxygen of the soul.

—MOSHE DAYAN

14 Timid men prefer the calm of despotism to the tempestuous sea of liberty.

—THOMAS JEFFERSON

15 We are in bondage to the law in order that we may be free.

—CICERO

1 To live anywhere in the world today and be against equality because of race or color is like living in Alaska and being against snow.

—WILLIAM FAULKNER
Essays, Speeches and Public Letters

2 The defect of equality is that we desire it only with our superiors.

—HENRY BECQUE

3 It is often easier to become outraged by injustice half a world away than by oppression and discrimination half a block from home.

—CARL T. ROWAN

TO PREVENT INJUSTICE . . .

4 There may be times when we are powerless to prevent injustice, but there must never be a time when we fail to protest.

—ELIE WIESEL

5 History will have to record that the greatest tragedy of this period of social transition was not the strident clamor of the bad people, but the appalling silence of the good people.

—REV. MARTIN LUTHER KING JR.
Stride Toward Freedom

6 There is no happiness for people at the expense of other people.

—ANWAR EL-SADAT

7 Injustice anywhere is a threat to justice everywhere.

—REV. MARTIN LUTHER KING JR.

8 Equal rights for the sexes will be achieved only when mediocre women occupy high positions.

—FRANÇOISE GIROUD

9 To do injustice is more disgraceful than to suffer it.

—PLATO

10 A great many people in this country are worried about law-and-order. And a great many people are worried about justice. But one thing is certain: you cannot have either until you have both.

—RAMSEY CLARK

11 What is morally wrong cannot be politically right.

—WILLIAM GLADSTONE

12 In recognizing the humanity of our fellow beings, we pay ourselves the highest tribute.

—THURGOOD MARSHALL

13 As long as you keep a person down, some part of you has to be down there to hold him down, so it means you cannot soar as you otherwise might.

—MARIAN ANDERSON

1 One man cannot hold another man down in the ditch without remaining down in the ditch with him.

—BOOKER T. WASHINGTON

2 Justice may be blind, but she has very sophisticated listening devices.

—EDGAR ARGO
in *Funny Times*

3 Justice is the insurance we have on our lives, and obedience is the premium we pay for it.

—WILLIAM PENN

4 A minority group has "arrived" only when it has the right to produce some fools and scoundrels without the entire group paying for it.

—CARL T. ROWAN

5 We are not bitter, not because we have forgiven but because there is so much to be done that we cannot afford to waste valuable time and resources on anger.

—GOVAN MBEKI
Johannesburg Weekly Mail (South Africa)

6 Efficiency can never be substituted for due process. Is not a dictatorship the more "efficient" form of government?

—THURGOOD MARSHALL

7 It is better to risk saving a guilty man than to condemn an innocent one.

—VOLTAIRE

8 Most lawyers who win a case advise their clients that "we have won" and, when justice has frowned upon their cause, that "you have lost."

—LOUIS NIZER

9 Injustice is relatively easy to bear; what stings is justice.

—H. L. MENCKEN
Prejudices

10 That old law about "an eye for an eye" leaves everybody blind.

—REV. MARTIN LUTHER KING JR.
Stride Toward Freedom

11 I would uphold the law if for no other reason but to protect myself.

—THOMAS MORE

12 I sometimes wish that people would put a little more emphasis upon the observance of the law than they do upon its enforcement.

—CALVIN COOLIDGE

13 The ultimate solution to the race problem lies in the willingness of men to obey the unenforceable.

—REV. MARTIN LUTHER KING JR.

1 The worst form of injustice is pretended justice.

—Plato

THE REAL BEAUTY OF DEMOCRACY . . .

2 The real beauty of democracy is that the average man believes he is above average.

—Morrie Brickman

3 Man's capacity for justice makes democracy possible, but man's inclination to injustice makes democracy necessary.

—Reinhold Niebuhr

4 Democracy's real test lies in its respect for minority opinion.

—Ellery Sedgwick
in *Jersey Journal*

5 The test of courage comes when we are in the minority. The test of tolerance comes when we are in the majority.

—Ralph W. Sockman

6 Consensus means that lots of people say collectively what nobody believes individually.

—Abba Eban
in *Montreal Gazette*

7 Democracy without morality is impossible.

—Jack Kemp

8 Democracy does not guarantee equality, only equality of opportunity.

—Irving Kristol

9 Democracy cannot survive without the guidance of a creative minority.

—Harlan F. Stone

10 One has the right to be wrong in a democracy.

—Claude Pepper

11 Democracy is a small hard core of common agreement, surrounded by a rich variety of individual differences.

—James B. Conant

12 Our political institutions work remarkably well. They are designed to clang against each other. The noise is democracy at work.

—Michael Novak

13 I like the noise of democracy.

—James Buchanan

14 Democracy, like any noncoercive relationship, rests on a shared understanding of limits.

—Elizabeth Drew
Washington Journal: The Events of 1973–1974

15 Democracy means that if the doorbell rings in the early hours, it is likely to be the milkman.

—Winston Churchill

1 Democracy is not a matter of sentiment, but of foresight. Any system that doesn't take the long run into account will burn itself out in the short run.

—CHARLES YOST

2 I'm tired of hearing it said that democracy doesn't work. Of course it doesn't work. We are supposed to work it.

—ALEXANDER WOOLLCOTT

3 People often say that, in a democracy, decisions are made by a majority of the people. Of course, that is not true. Decisions are made by a majority of those who make themselves heard and who vote—a very different thing.

—WALTER H. JUDD

4 Democracy, like love, can survive any attack—save neglect and indifference.

—PAUL SWEENEY

5 There can be no daily democracy without daily citizenship.

—RALPH NADER

6 Democracy is the only system that persists in asking the powers that be whether they are the powers that ought to be.

—SYDNEY J. HARRIS

7 Every private citizen has a public responsibility.

—MYRA JANCO DANIELS
in *Newsweek*

8 We will all be better citizens when voting records of our Congressmen are followed as carefully as scores of pro-football games.

—LOU ERICKSON
in *Atlanta Journal*

9 The most important political office is that of private citizen.

—LOUIS BRANDEIS

10 Democracy is based upon the conviction that there are extraordinary possibilities in ordinary people.

—HARRY EMERSON FOSDICK

11 Democracy is not a mathematical deduction proved once and for all time. Democracy is a just faith fervently held, a commitment to be tested again and again in the fiery furnace of history.

—JACK KEMP

12 Democracy may not prove in the long run to be as efficient as other forms of government, but it has one saving grace: it allows us to know and say that it isn't.

—BILL MOYERS
in *Newsweek*

1 Democracy is like a raft. It won't
sink, but you'll always have your
feet wet.

—Quoted by RUSSELL LONG in
The Washingtonian

2 Whenever you find yourself on
the side of the majority, it is time
to pause and reflect.

—MARK TWAIN

3 Sometimes a majority simply
means that all the fools are on the
same side.

—CLAUDE McDONALD

4 Democracy is the recurrent suspi-
cion that more than half of the
people are right more than half
of the time.

—E. B. WHITE
in *The New Yorker*

5 It's not the hand that signs the
laws that holds the destiny of
America. It's the hand that casts
the ballot.

—HARRY TRUMAN

6 It's not the voting that's democracy;
it's the counting.

—TOM STOPPARD
Jumpers

7 Anything that keeps a politician
humble is healthy for democracy.

—MICHAEL KINSLEY

8 Democracy is the art of disciplin-
ing oneself so that one need not
be disciplined by others.

—GEORGES CLEMENCEAU

IN POLITICS . . .

9 In politics, what begins in fear
usually ends in folly.

—SAMUEL TAYLOR COLERIDGE

10 The bedfellows politics makes are
never strange. It only seems that
way to those who have not
watched the courtship.

—KIRKPATRICK SALE

11 Politics has got so expensive that
it takes lots of money to even get
beat with nowadays.

—WILL ROGERS

12 Politicians and journalists share
the same fate in that they often
understand tomorrow the things
they talk about today.

—HELMUT SCHMIDT

13 Politics is like coaching a football
team. You have to be smart
enough to understand the game
but not smart enough to lose
interest.

—EUGENE McCARTHY

1 No man should enter politics unless he is either independently rich or independently poor.

—ROBERT JAMES MANION
Gentlemen, Players and Politicians

2 The idea that you can merchandise candidates for high office like breakfast cereal is the ultimate indignity to the democratic process.

—ADLAI E. STEVENSON

3 Politics is perhaps the only profession for which no preparation is thought necessary.

—ROBERT LOUIS STEVENSON

4 The truly skillful politician is one who, when he comes to a fork in the road, goes both ways.

—MARCO A. ALMAZAN
Píldoras Anticonceptistas

5 What's real in politics is what the voters decide is real.

—BEN J. WATTENBERG
Values Matter Most

6 Politics are too serious a matter to be left to the politicians.

—GEN. CHARLES DE GAULLE

7 Everything is changing. People are taking their comedians seriously and the politicians as a joke.

—WILL ROGERS

8 When things don't go well they like to blame presidents; and that's something that presidents are paid for.

—JOHN F. KENNEDY

9 Sincerity and competence is a strong combination. In politics, it's everything.

—PEGGY NOONAN
in *Catholic New York*

10 When a man assumes a public trust he should consider himself as public property.

—THOMAS JEFFERSON

11 Talk is cheap—except when Congress does it.

—CULLEN HIGHTOWER

12 A strong conviction that something must be done is the parent of many bad measures.

—DANIEL WEBSTER

13 Those who corrupt the public mind are just as evil as those who steal from the public purse.

—ADLAI E. STEVENSON

14 When the search for truth is confused with political advocacy, the pursuit of knowledge is reduced to the quest for power.

—ALSTON CHASE
In a Dark Wood

1 A statesman who keeps his ear permanently glued to the ground will have neither elegance of posture nor flexibility of movement.
—ABBA EBAN

2 Congress is continually appointing fact-finding committees, when what we really need are some fact-facing committees.
—ROGER ALLEN
in *Grand Rapids Press*

3 Asking an incumbent member of Congress to vote for term limits is a bit like asking a chicken to vote for Colonel Sanders.
—BOB INGLIS

4 A politician without a prepared text is like a Boris Becker without a tennis racket, a dog biscuit without a dog, or opera glasses without an opera.
—C. M. BOWRA

5 When buying and selling are controlled by legislation, the first things to be bought and sold are legislators.
—P. J. O'ROURKE

6 Now and then an innocent man is sent to the legislature.
—KIN HUBBARD

7 Election year is that period when politicians get free speech mixed up with cheap talk.
—J. B. KIDD

8 Politicians are like ships: noisiest when lost in a fog.
—BENNETT CERF

9 A politician is a person who can make waves and then make you think he's the only one who can save the ship.
—IVERN BALL
in *Modern Secretary*

10 Politicians say they're beefing up our economy. Most don't know beef from pork.
—HAROLD LOWMAN

11 Politicians are people who, when they see light at the end of the tunnel, go out and buy some more tunnel.
—JOHN QUINTON

12 It's extremely difficult to build a political platform that supports candidates without holding up taxpayers.
—HAROLD COFFIN

13 Washington is a place where politicians don't know which way is up and taxes don't know which way is down.
—ROBERT ORBEN
in *The Wall Street Journal*

1 Politics is the art of getting money from the rich and votes from the poor, with the pretext of protecting one from the other.

—*Muy Interesante*

2 Instead of giving a politician the keys to the city, it might be better to change the locks.

—DOUG LARSON

3 To create a housing shortage in a huge country, heavily wooded, with a small population—ah, that's proof of pure political genius.

—RICHARD J. NEEDHAM
The Globe and Mail (Toronto)

4 When they call the roll in the Senate, the Senators do not know whether to answer "Present" or "Not guilty."

—THEODORE ROOSEVELT

IF A GOVERNMENT COMMISSION HAD WORKED ON THE HORSE . . .

5 If a government commission had worked on the horse, you would have had the first horse that could operate its knee joint in both directions. The only trouble is it couldn't have stood up.

—PETER DRUCKER

6 Bureaucracy is the art of making the possible impossible.

—JAVIER PASCUAL SALCEDO

7 I don't make jokes. I just watch the government and report the facts.

—WILL ROGERS

8 Governing a large country is like frying a small fish. You spoil it with too much poking.

—LAO-TZU

9 A little government and a little luck are necessary in life, but only a fool trusts either of them.

—P. J. O'ROURKE
Parliament of Whores

10 Everyone wants to live at the expense of the state. They forget that the state wants to live at the expense of everyone.

—FRÉDÉRIC BASTIAT

11 Government can't give us anything without depriving us of something else.

—HENRY HAZLITT
in *The Freeman*

12 Everybody wants to eat at the government's table, but nobody wants to do the dishes.

—WERNER FINCK

1 When government accepts responsibility for people, then people no longer take responsibility for themselves.

—GEORGE PATAKI

2 The mistakes made by Congress wouldn't be so bad if the next Congress didn't keep trying to correct them.

—CULLEN HIGHTOWER

3 Useless laws weaken the necessary laws.

—MONTESQUIEU

4 Bad laws are the worst sort of tyranny.

—EDMUND BURKE

5 You are better off not knowing how sausages and laws are made.

—Washington, D.C., adage

6 A country is considered the more civilized the more the wisdom and efficiency of its laws hinder a weak man from becoming too weak or a powerful one too powerful.

—PRIMO LEVI
Survival In Auschwitz

7 Government never furthered any enterprise but by the alacrity with which it got out of its way.

—HENRY DAVID THOREAU

A government is the only vessel 8 known to leak from the top.

—JAMES RESTON
in *The New York Times*

Knowing exactly how much of the 9 future can be introduced into the present is the secret of a great government.

—VICTOR HUGO

It's every American's duty to support his government, but not necessarily in the style to which it has become accustomed. 10

—Quoted by Thomas Clifford

The best defense against usurpatory government is an assertive citizenry. 11

—WILLIAM F. BUCKLEY JR.
Windfall: The End of the Affair

We should know everything we 12 can about government — and the first thing we should know is what we're paying for it.

—ROBERT FULFORD
Financial Times

Government investigations have 13 always contributed more to our amusement than they have to our knowledge.

—WILL ROGERS

1 It's one thing to call a spade a spade, but I wish my local social security office hadn't called the maternity benefit a lump sum.
—JOHN WATTS

2 There's nothing wrong with waiting for your ship to come in, but you can be sure that if it ever does, the Receiver of Revenue will be right there to help you unload it.
—DAVID BIGGS
Cape Town Argus (South Africa)

3 What is the difference between a taxidermist and a tax collector? The taxidermist takes only your skin.
—MARK TWAIN

4 Tax reform is taking the taxes off things that have been taxed in the past and putting taxes on things that haven't been taxed before.
—ART BUCHWALD

5 The government deficit is the difference between the amount of money the government spends and the amount it has the nerve to collect.
—SAM EWING

FINANCE IS THE ART . . .

6 Finance is the art of passing currency from hand to hand until it finally disappears.
—ROBERT W. SARNOFF

7 Money still talks, but it has to catch its breath more often.
—*Parts Pups*

8 Money talks—but credit has an echo.
—BOB THAVES

9 A big disappointment in life is the discovery that the man who writes the finance company ads isn't the one who makes the loans.
—*The London Free Press* (Ontario)

10 Time was when the average person could pay as he goes. Nowadays he has to pay as he comes and goes.
—O. A. BATTISTA

11 An economist is an expert who will know tomorrow why the things he predicted yesterday didn't happen.
—EARL WILSON

12 Economics is extremely useful as a form of employment for economists.
—JOHN KENNETH GALBRAITH

1 The economy depends about as much on economists as the weather does on weather forecasters.

—Jean-Paul Kauffmann

2 An economist's guess is liable to be just as good as anybody else's.

—Will Rogers

3 Isn't it strange? The same people who laugh at Gypsy fortunetellers take economists seriously.

—The Cincinnati Enquirer

4 The only function of economic forecasting is to make astrology look respectable.

—Ezra Solomon

5 We have become, to some extent, economic hypochondriacs. You get a wiggle in a statistic, and everyone runs to get the thermometer.

—Paul W. McCracken

6 Torture numbers, and they'll confess to anything.

—Gregg Easterbrook
in The New Republic

7 Although he may not always recognize his bondage, modern man lives under a tyranny of numbers.

—Nicholas Eberstadt
The Tyranny of Numbers:
Mismeasurement and Misrule

8 It is not the employer who pays— he only handles the money. It is the product that pays wages.

—Henry Ford

9 It would be nice if the poor were to get even half of the money that is spent in studying them.

—Bill Vaughan

10 To view poverty simply as an economic condition, to be measured by statistics, is simplistic, misleading and false; poverty is a state of mind, a matter of horizons.

—Patrick J. Buchanan
Right from the Beginning

11 When economics gets important enough, it becomes political.

—Peter G. Peterson

12 Statistics are human beings with the tears wiped off.

—Paul Brodeur
Outrageous Misconduct

13 When goods do not cross borders, soldiers will.

—Frédéric Bastiat

14 There are so many men who can figure costs, and so few who can measure values.

—Tribune (San Marino, California)

15 Only a fool thinks price and value are the same.

—Antonio Machado

1 The best cure for the national economy would be economy.
—ASHLEY COOPER
in *News and Courier* (Charleston, South Carolina)

2 People want economy, and they will pay any price to get it.
—LEE IACOCCA

3 The shortest recorded period of time lies between the minute you put some money away for a rainy day and the unexpected arrival of rain.
—JANE BRYANT QUINN

4 One thing I could never abide was the leaving of money to lie idle, or even to have credit and not use it.
—LORD THOMSON OF FLEET
After I Was Sixty

5 Measure wealth not by the things you have, but by the things you have for which you would not take money.
—ANONYMOUS

6 Money changes people just as often as it changes hands.
—AL BATT

7 The most efficient labor-saving device is still money.
—FRANKLIN P. JONES

8 Money does make all the difference. If you have two jobs and you're rich, you have diversified interests. If you have two jobs and you're poor, you're moonlighting.
—*Changing Times*

9 Money is better than poverty, if only for financial reasons.
—WOODY ALLEN

10 A rand goes a long way these days. You can carry it around for days without finding a thing it will buy.
—*Daily Dispatch*
(East London, South Africa)

11 I don't like money, actually, but it quiets my nerves.
—JOE LOUIS

12 Money is a good servant but a bad master.
—FRENCH PROVERB

13 The beauty of having a low income is that there is not enough money to buy what you don't really need.
—RAY INMAN

14 There is nothing so habit-forming as money.
—DON MARQUIS

15 When a man says money can do anything, that settles it; he hasn't any.
—ED HOWE

1 Bankruptcy stared me in the face, but one thought kept me calm; soon I'd be too poor to need an anti-theft alarm.

—GINA ROTHFELS

To live in society . . .

2 To live in society doesn't mean simply living side by side with others in a more or less close cohesion; it means living through one another and for one another.

—PAUL-EUGENE ROY

3 Civilization is a process whose purpose is to combine single human individuals, and after that families, and then races, peoples and nations, into one great unity, the unity of mankind.

—*The Complete Psychological Works of* SIGMUND FREUD

4 We ought to think that we are one of the leaves of a tree, and the tree is all humanity. We cannot live without the others, without the tree.

—PABLO CASALS

5 A community is like a ship; everyone ought to be prepared to take the helm.

—HENRIK IBSEN

6 No one is rich enough to do without a neighbor.

—HAROLD HELFER

7 A school system without parents at its foundation is just like a bucket with a hole in it.

—REV. JESSE L. JACKSON

8 If we cannot now end our differences, at least we can help make the world safe for diversity.

—JOHN F. KENNEDY

9 Aristide Briand, French statesman and winner of the Nobel Peace Prize: "In order to have peace we must want it, and not always doubt it."

—MATTHIAS JAGGI
Schweizer Jugend

10 There's just no place you can go any longer and escape the global problems, so one's thinking must become global.

—THEODORE ROSZAK

11 In every community, there is work to be done. In every nation, there are wounds to heal. In every heart, there is the power to do it.

—MARIANNE WILLIAMSON
A Return to Love

1 A nation is a body of people who
have done great things together
in the past and who hope to do
great things together in the future.
　　　　　　　　　—F. H. UNDERHILL
　　　Colombo's Little Book of Canadian
　Proverbs, Graffiti, Limericks and Other
　　　　　　　　　　　　　Vital Matters

2 I look to a time when brotherhood needs no publicity, to a time
when a brotherhood award would
be as ridiculous as an award for
getting up each morning.
　　　　　　　　　—DANIEL D. MICH

3 We should see the new world
order as a building constructed
brick by brick and be motivated
by the fact that we have only got
as far as building the ground floor.
　　　　　　　　　—DOUGLAS HURD
　　　　　　　Daily Telegraph (London)

4 I can think of no more stirring
symbol of man's humanity to man
than a fire engine.
　　　　　　　　　—KURT VONNEGUT

WHOEVER DOESN'T KNOW
THE PAST . . .

5 Whoever doesn't know the past
must have little understanding of
the present and no vision of the
future.
　　　　　　　　　—JOSEPH S. RAYMOND

History is the unfolding of　　　6
miscalculation.
　　　　　　　　　—BARBARA TUCHMAN

History doesn't pass the dishes　　7
again.
　　　　　　　　　—LOUIS-FERDINAND CÉLINE

History is a vast early-warning　　8
system.
　　　　　　　　　—NORMAN COUSINS

History is a better guide than　　9
good intentions.
　　　　　　　　　—JEANE J. KIRKPATRICK

Once the game is over, the king　10
and the pawn go back into the
same box.
　　　　　　　　　—ITALIAN PROVERB

A nation forgetful and disrespect-　11
ful of its past has no future, and
deserves none.
　　　　　　　—Daily Telegraph (London)

Righteousness is easy in　　　12
retrospect.
　　　　　　　　　—ARTHUR SCHLESINGER JR.
　　　　　　　　　　　　in Newsweek

The history of every country　　13
begins in the heart of a man or
a woman.
　　　　　　　　　—WILLA CATHER

1 To understand a man, you must know his memories. The same is true of a nation.

—ANTHONY QUAYLE

2 It was the same with those old birds in Greece and Rome as it is now. The only thing new in the world is the history you don't know.

—HARRY S. TRUMAN

3 I look upon the whole world as my fatherland, and every war has to me the horror of a family feud.

—HELEN KELLER
in *New York Call*

4 Genuine tragedies in the world are not conflicts between right and wrong. They are conflicts between two rights.

—GEORG HEGEL

5 Nationalism is an infantile disease. It is the measles of mankind.

—ALBERT EINSTEIN

6 In individuals, insanity is rare; but in groups, parties, nations and epochs, it is the rule.

—FRIEDRICH NIETZSCHE

7 The great tragedies of history occur not when right confronts wrong but when two rights confront each other.

—HENRY A. KISSINGER

8 We have war when at least one of the parties to a conflict wants something more than it wants peace.

—JEANE J. KIRKPATRICK

9 In war, there are no unwounded soldiers.

—JOSÉ NAROSKY

10 The soldiers fight, and the kings are heroes.

—BARBARA MECHELS

11 When elephants fight, it's the grass that suffers.

—AFRICAN PROVERB

12 Might does not make right; it only makes history.

—JIM FIEBIG

13 In war there is no second prize for the runner-up.

—GEN. OMAR N. BRADLEY

14 As long as war is regarded as wicked, it will always have its fascination. When it is looked upon as vulgar, it will cease to be popular.

—OSCAR WILDE

15 You can build a throne with bayonets, but you can't sit on it for long.

—BORIS YELTSIN

1 A peace which depends upon fear is nothing but a suppressed war.
—HENRY VAN DYKE

2 Foreign relations are like human relations. They are endless. The solution of one problem usually leads to another.
—JAMES RESTON

3 Treaties are like roses and young girls. They last while they last.
—CHARLES DE GAULLE

4 Revolutions are built on empty bellies.
—WYNDHAM HARTLEY
Natal Witness (South Africa)

5 Who overcomes by force hath overcome but half his foe.
—JOHN MILTON

6 I like a little rebellion now and then. It is like a storm in the atmosphere.
—THOMAS JEFFERSON

7 No one is more surprised than a revolutionary rebelled against.
—PIERRE GAXOTTE

8 Every successful revolution puts on in time the robes of the tyrant it has deposed.
—BARBARA TUCHMAN

9 If we want things to stay as they are, things will have to change.
—GIUSEPPE TOMASI DI LAMPEDUSA
The Leopard

10 It is not necessary to imagine the world ending in fire or ice. There are two other possibilities: one is paper work, and the other is nostalgia.
—FRANK ZAPPA

11 Perhaps the rediscovery of our humanity, and the potential of the human spirit which we have read about in legends of older civilizations, or in accounts of solitary mystics, or in tales of science fiction writers— perhaps this will constitute the true revolution of the future. The new frontier lies not beyond the planets but within each one of us.
—PIERRE ELLIOT TRUDEAU
Biodynamics